PUFFIN BOOKS

THE BOURNVITA QUIZ CONTEST
COLLECTOR'S EDITION: VOLUME 1

Derek O'Brien is an author, television personality, public speaker, politician and quizmaster.

Born in Kolkata, he began his career as a journalist for *Sportsworld* magazine but soon shifted to advertising. After working for a number of very successful years as creative head of Ogilvy, Derek decided to focus all his energy and talent on his passion—quizzing.

Today, Derek is Asia's best known quizmaster and the CEO of Derek O'Brien & Associates. He has been the host of the longest-running game show on Indian television, the *Bournvita Quiz Contest*, for which he was voted Best Anchor of a Game Show at the Indian Television Academy Awards three years in a row. Always innovating, Derek is also credited with having conducted the first quiz on Twitter in 2010.

Derek O'Brien is a twice-serving member of the Rajya Sabha from West Bengal. He is the parliamentary party leader of the All India Trinamool Congress in the Rajya Sabha as well as the chief national spokesperson of the party. He has spoken at, among others, Harvard, Yale and Columbia universities in the US as well as several IIMs, IITs and other premier educational institutions in India. He addressed the United Nations General Assembly as a member of the Indian parliamentary delegation in 2012. He has written over sixty bestselling reference, quiz and school textbooks.

To know more about the author, visit his website www.derek.in. You can also follow him on Twitter, Instagram and Facebook (@derekobrienmp).

READ MORE IN PUFFIN BY THE SAME AUTHOR

Discover with Derek (Primer, Parts I–III)
Cadbury Bournvita Book of Knowledge (Books 1–14)
The Best of Cadbury Bournvita Quiz Contest
The Puffin Factfinder

THE

COLLECTOR'S EDITION
VOLUME 1

DEREK O'BRIEN

PUFFIN BOOKS
An imprint of Penguin Random House

PUFFIN BOOKS

USA | Canada | UK | Ireland | Australia
New Zealand | India | South Africa | China | Singapore

Puffin Books is part of the Penguin Random House group of companies
whose addresses can be found at global.penguinrandomhouse.com

Published by Penguin Random House India Pvt. Ltd
4th Floor, Capital Tower 1, MG Road,
Gurugram 122 002, Haryana, India

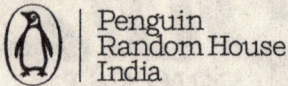

First published in Puffin Books by Penguin Random House India 2019

10 9 8 7 6 5 4 3 2

The views and opinions expressed in this book are the author's own and the
facts are as reported by him which have been verified to the extent possible,
and the publishers are not in any way liable for the same.

ISBN 9780143447009

Typeset in Bauer Grotesk Pro by Manipal Digital Systems, Manipal
Book design by Parag Chitale
Printed at Repro India Limited

www.penguin.co.in

This is a legitimate digitally printed version of the book and therefore might not
have certain extra finishing on the cover.

CONTENTS

A BEAUTIFUL JOURNEY

A HISTORY OF THE *BOURNVITA QUIZ CONTEST*
BY DEREK O'BRIEN

The Bournvita Quiz Contest is a milestone in the history of radio and television in India. In its long journey of more than forty-five years, the programme has entertained, inspired and shaped the lives of millions of schoolchildren across India and the Gulf countries.

The quiz started as a radio programme in 1972, with the legendary Hamid Sayani as quizmaster. A few years later, following his sudden death, his brother, Ameen Sayani, took over. Ameen Sayani, with his booming voice and inimitable style, took BQC to another level. It became one of the most popular English-language programmes on Vividh Bharati. Listeners all over India made tuning in a Sunday habit.

My association with the quiz started in the early 1990s. In 1992, Cadbury's sponsorship of the *Bournvita Quiz Contest* on radio came to an end, and the company wanted me to conduct fifty stage quizzes in five cities. The fee was Rs 2.5 lakh for the year.

In 1994, Cadbury told me it was not going to renew the contract. It had decided to take the programme to television and was discontinuing the stage quizzes. The television quiz would be designed and shot by a production house in Mumbai. It would hire a presenter and outsource the question setting to a third party. As a quiz professional, I knew the three aspects could not be compartmentalized. This formula would not work.

Soon Cadbury and the production house realized this too, and asked me to set the questions. I refused to do it for another presenter, who would simply read from a script. Either I would set the questions and be the quizmaster, or I wanted no part of it. Reluctantly Cadbury agreed—but I would need to do a screen test. After all those years of conducting quizzes, I went to a Mumbai studio for the test. It was a nervous moment, but I passed.

Next, Rila Banerjee and I were hired, on behalf of our company, to go to Mumbai, research and set the questions and have me present the show. I was paid Rs 5000 per show. In 1994, it seemed a big amount.

A year down the line, the technical crew working with the production house realized that Rila and I were running the show. Gyan Sahay and Dongrej Gor came to us on behalf of the crew to say, 'Take over the quiz. Do a contract with Cadbury. We'll work for you.' So, from 1995, BQC became entirely our baby. It was the third flagship show on Zee TV—alongside Rajat Sharma's *Aap ki Adalat* and Annu Kapoor's *Antakshari*. Our show later moved to Sony Entertainment Television.

Having been off the air for a few years, the *Bournvita Quiz Contest* made a comeback in 2011 after 'Bring BQC Back', an overwhelming movement on social networking sites, stormed cyberspace. Cadbury India Limited and Derek O'Brien & Associates responded to the call.

The new *Bournvita Quiz Contest* was bilingual—in English and Hindi—with the super-talented Saumya Tandon as my co-quizmaster. This time the quiz was aired on Colors.

The still growing popularity of BQC led to the show being launched in Tamil in 2013, with my young and bubbly co-host Nisha Krishnan helping me take baby steps in Tamil on Sun TV.

Keeping with the times, and to meet the demands of the digital age, in 2015 the show moved from television to YouTube, and in the following year, became an exclusive mobile app.

As exciting as the television shows were the city finals that we conducted in a hundred cities, hosted by my colleagues from Derek O'Brien & Associates, in order to select participants for the TV show.

Over the years, more than 2000 schools from different parts of the country have participated in the quiz. Many schools from Dubai, Muscat, Abu Dhabi, Sharjah, Kuwait and Qatar have also been a part of this iconic programme, which has consistently provided wholesome edutainment—education and entertainment. A number of celebrities from the fields of cinema, music, sports and politics have also made special appearances on the show.

But the true heroes and torchbearers of this iconic quiz show in the past two decades were not us, but the principals, teachers, parents and students who gave us their unending support.

Thank you ever so much for being a part of this glorious journey, for helping us take the *Bournvita Quiz Contest* to such great heights and for joining us in our continual quest of 'making knowledge interesting to help people grow'.

ANIMAL KINGDOM

1. Why do bees perform a complicated movement called the waggle dance?
   a) To teach young bees to fly
   b) To tell other bees where to find food
   c) To warn other bees about other hives
   d) To attract other bees

2. Which are the only big cats to live in groups called prides?
   a) Lions
   b) Tigers
   c) Jaguars
   d) Cheetahs

3. Which animal secretes a reddish oily fluid sometimes called blood sweat?
   a) Zebra
   b) Elephant

    c) Rhinoceros
    d) Hippopotamus

4. Monarch, Red Admiral, Green Hairstreak, Grayling are types of . . .
    a) Hummingbirds
    b) Butterflies
    c) Snakes
    d) Jellyfish

5. What is the national heritage animal of India?
    a) Lion
    b) Elephant
    c) Deer
    d) Camel

6. The famous Keibul Lamjao National Park in Manipur is . . .
    a) The only floating national park in the world
    b) The highest national park in the world
    c) The only place where Asiatic lions are found
    d) The oldest national park in India

7. Which snake, unlike all other snakes, builds nests for its young ones?
    a) Pit viper
    b) Green anaconda
    c) Python
    d) King cobra

8. The venomous black widow is a species of . . .
   a) Scorpion
   b) Mosquito
   c) Spider
   d) Ant

9. The name of which animal comes from a Sanskrit word meaning 'the spotted one'?
   a) Cheetah
   b) Jaguar
   c) Giraffe
   d) Zebra

10. A rabbit's tail is called a scut. What is a fox's bushy tail called?
   a) Cuff
   b) Cluster
   c) Nib
   d) Brush

11. Cuttlefish have . . .
   a) W-shaped pupils
   b) Twelve stomachs
   c) Fourteen hearts
   d) Hourglass-shaped shells

12. Which is the largest tree-dwelling animal in the world?
   a) Orangutan
   b) Spotted owl
   c) Lemur
   d) Koala

13. Which breed of dog was referred to as 'sleeve dog' because it was carried by Chinese royalty in the sleeves of their robes?
a) Saluki
b) Chihuahua
c) Pekingese
d) Poodle

14. The duck-billed platypus and the echidna or spiny anteater are the only two mammals that . . .
a) Lay eggs
b) Sting
c) Are cold-blooded
d) Fly

15. The dodo is an extinct bird of . . .
a) Mauritius
b) New Zealand
c) India
d) Chile

16. Male seahorses have the remarkable ability to . . .
a) Carry the eggs and give birth to young ones
b) Live on both land and water
c) Change their shape in danger
d) Survive without food for five years

17. A species of which of these is thought to be the most intelligent of all invertebrate animals?
a) Housefly
b) Jellyfish

c) Octopus
d) Snail

18. If you saw a *hangul* in Kashmir, what would you have spotted?
a) A yak
b) A stag
c) A bear
d) A snake

19. A tigon is the offspring of a male tiger and a lioness. What do you call the offspring of a male lion and a tigress?
a) Ligon
b) Ligress
c) Litiger
d) Liger

20. Which of these is a kind of bookworm?
a) Ragfish
b) Catfish
c) Jellyfish
d) Silverfish

ART AND CULTURE

1. According to legend, which painter is believed to have designed the uniforms of the Swiss Guards of Vatican City?
   a) Van Gogh
   b) Leonardo da Vinci
   c) Michelangelo
   d) Rembrandt

2. In the 1920s, who invited Atomba Singh to teach Manipuri dance in Bengal?
   a) Rabindranath Tagore
   b) Swami Vivekananda
   c) Satyajit Ray
   d) Sri Aurobindo

3. Which of these is a famous bronze sculpture by Auguste Rodin?
   a) *The Creator*
   b) *The Thinker*

c) *The Performer*
d) *The Destroyer*

4. What are murals painted on?
   a) Walls
   b) Clothes
   c) Flowerpots
   d) Books

5. Which painter's autobiography is titled *Pandharpur ka Ek Ladka?*
   a) Manjit Bawa
   b) Satish Gujral
   c) M.F. Husain
   d) Tyeb Mehta

6. In Kerala, a Yakshagana performance starts and ends with a prayer to which god?
   a) Ganesha
   b) Rama
   c) Indra
   d) Brahma

7. In the batik method of dyeing, patterned parts are traditionally covered with which substance so that they do not receive colour?
   a) Sugar
   b) Wax
   c) Salt
   d) Lac

8. In Kathakali, how would you identify a person playing a noble male character?
   a) His face would be painted green.
   b) He would be wearing a red beard.
   c) His face would be painted white.
   d) He would be wearing a black beard.

9. Who founded the Kalakshetra Foundation in Chennai to preserve and popularize Bharatanatyam?
   a) T. Balasaraswati
   b) Rukmini Devi Arundale
   c) Protima Bedi
   d) Hema Malini

10. Madhubani paintings are named after . . .
   a) Their use of easy brushstrokes
   b) A district in Bihar
   c) The main ingredient used in making colours
   d) One of the 108 names of Sita

11. Origami involves . . .
   a) Painting directly on a canvas
   b) Writing and scratching on a wall
   c) Applying small pieces of fabric to a bigger piece
   d) Folding paper to make interesting things

12. Odhra Magadha is the earliest form of which Indian dance form?
   a) Kuchipudi
   b) Kathak

c) Odissi

d) Kathakali

13. *The Last Supper*, a painting by Leonardo da Vinci, depicts . . .
   a) Jesus Christ with his disciples
   b) A lady named Lisa del Giocondo
   c) Café Terrace at Night
   d) The Potato Eaters

14. Which art form from Persia was introduced in Rajasthan under the patronage of Maharaja Sawai Ram Singh II?
   a) Batik
   b) Filigree
   c) Blue pottery
   d) Chikankari

15. Bidriware derives its name from the town of Bidar. In which state is Bidar located?
   a) Karnataka
   b) Kerala
   c) Gujarat
   d) Odisha

16. Whom did Nand Das base his initial plays of the Rasleela on?
   a) Hanuman
   b) Krishna
   c) Rama
   d) Shiva

17. Which of these words comes from two Persian words meaning 'gold' and 'embroidery'?
a) Tangaliya
b) Kasuti
c) Zardozi
d) Chikankari

18. Lachhu Maharaj, Birju Maharaj and Shambhu Maharaj were exponents of which classical dance form?
a) Odissi
b) Kathak
c) Kuchipudi
d) Kathakali

19. This art form was developed about 300 kilometres from Chennai. It uses gold leaf as well as precious and semi-precious stones liberally. Name it.
a) Tanjore painting
b) Warli painting
c) Madhubani painting
d) Pattachitra painting

20. What term is used to describe words or drawings scribbled illicitly on a wall in a public place?
a) Tempera
b) Baroque
c) Collage
d) Graffiti

ASTRONOMY

1. Armalcolite, a mineral found on the moon, is named after . . .
   a) Argon, manganese and cobalt—the chief components of armalcolite
   b) Artemis, the goddess of the moon
   c) The three Apollo 11 astronauts—Armstrong, Aldrin and Collins
   d) The armadillo

2. Who discovered the four largest moons of Jupiter—Io, Europa, Ganymede and Callisto?
   a) William Herschel
   b) Galileo Galilei
   c) Johannes Kepler
   d) Isaac Newton

3. What kind of animal was Laika, the first animal to be sent into space?
a) Monkey
b) Guinea pig
c) Dog
d) Mouse

4. Which star is closest to the earth?
a) Sirius
b) Polaris
c) The sun
d) Vega

5. Who was the first person to propose that the sun is at the centre of the universe, with the planets moving around it?
a) Nicolaus Copernicus
b) William Herschel
c) Johannes Kepler
d) Tycho Brahe

6. Collectively, how many moons do the planets Mercury and Venus have?
a) One
b) Two
c) Three
d) None

7. The word 'comet' comes from a Greek word meaning ...
a) Hot-headed
b) Long-haired

c) Big-mouthed
d) Large-hearted

8. Olympus Mons is . . .
    a) The largest volcano on Mars and also in the solar system
    b) The spot where Neil Armstrong set foot on the moon
    c) The largest moon of Jupiter
    d) The biggest known ring of Saturn

9. Liberty, Equality and Fraternity are the arcs of a ring of which planet?
    a) Saturn
    b) Neptune
    c) Uranus
    d) Venus

10. The birth and death of Mark Twain coincided with . . .
    a) The appearance of Halley's Comet
    b) The discovery of Uranus and Neptune
    c) The birth and death of Edmond Halley
    d) A total solar eclipse

11. Which is the furthest planet from the earth that can be seen by the unaided human eye?
    a) Mercury
    b) Saturn
    c) Jupiter
    d) Neptune

12. At which Indian landmark would you find instruments named Samrat Yantra, Jai Prakash Yantra and Dhruva Darshak Pattika?

a) Gol Gumbaz, Vijayapura
b) Jantar Mantar, Jaipur
c) Purana Qila, New Delhi
d) Golconda Fort, Hyderabad

13. When Indira Gandhi asked what India looked like from space, what did Rakesh Sharma say?

a) 'Atulya Bharat.'
b) 'Saare jahaan se achcha.'
c) 'Satyam shivam sundaram.'
d) 'Mera Bharat mahaan.'

14. The satellites of Uranus are named after . . .

a) Roman gods and goddesses
b) Characters from the works of Alexander Pope and Shakespeare
c) Kings and queens of the United Kingdom
d) Flowers

15. In the Western zodiac, which constellation is represented by the scales?

a) Libra
b) Virgo
c) Leo
d) Scorpio

16. Sirius, the brightest star in the night sky, is also called the . . .
   a) Horse Star
   b) Cat Star
   c) Bear Star
   d) Dog Star

17. The first satellite completely designed and fabricated in India was named after . . .
   a) Bhaskara
   b) Aryabhata
   c) Varahamihira
   d) Brahmagupta

18. In the 1920s, Edwin Powell Hubble established that the Andromeda was a . . .
   a) Dwarf planet closest to the earth
   b) Satellite of Jupiter
   c) Separate galaxy beyond the Milky Way
   d) Black hole

19. Who was the first woman of Indian origin in space?
   a) Kalpana Chawla
   b) Bachendri Pal
   c) Sunita Williams
   d) Kiran Bedi

20. The Greeks referred to which planet as Apollo in the morning and Hermes in the evening?
   a) Mercury
   b) Venus
   c) Earth
   d) Mars

AWARDS

1. Which Indian was nominated for the Nobel Peace Prize in 1937, 1938, 1939, 1947 and 1948 but was never awarded the prize?
   a) Subhas Chandra Bose
   b) Jawaharlal Nehru
   c) J.R.D. Tata
   d) Mahatma Gandhi

2. The Bharat Ratna award is designed in the shape of . . .
   a) A peepul leaf
   b) Indra's vajra
   c) The sun
   d) A lotus

3. In 1976, which was the only category in which the film *Sholay* received the Filmfare Award?
   a) Best direction

b) Best music
c) Best editing
d) Best choreography

4. In what way was Richard Hadlee's knighthood different from that of other cricketers?
   a) He was the first cricketer to be knighted while still playing the game.
   b) He was knighted but not for his contribution to the sport.
   c) He did not want the knighthood but had to accept it because of his country's prime minister.
   d) He was the first cricketer to be knighted before starting his cricketing career.

5. On a Param Vir Chakra medal, the words 'Param Vir Chakra' are written in two languages. Which two?
   a) Hindi and Tamil
   b) Hindi and English
   c) Hindi and Sanskrit
   d) English and Sanskrit

6. In 1954, the Bharat Ratna was awarded for the first time. Two of the first three recipients were S. Radhakrishnan and C. Rajagopalachari. Who was the third?
   a) C.V. Raman
   b) Ravi Shankar
   c) M. Visvesvaraya
   d) Satyajit Ray

7. Who was the first recipient of the Dadasaheb Phalke Award?
   a) Devika Rani

b) Sulochana
c) Kanan Devi
d) Durga Khote

8. In 2006, Kiran Desai created a record when she won the Man Booker Prize. She became the ...
a) Youngest person to win the prize
b) First Indian to win the prize
c) First winner for a debut novel
d) First person to win two years in a row

9. Which of these awards includes a cash prize, a citation and a bronze replica of the goddess Vagdevi?
a) Sahitya Akademi Award
b) Dronacharya Award
c) Tansen Samman
d) Jnanpith Award

10. In the USA, the Newbery Medal is awarded for contribution to which specific field of literature?
a) Historical fiction
b) Crime fiction
c) Children's literature
d) Science fiction

11. Who received the United Nations (UN) Population Award in 1992?
a) Rajiv Gandhi
b) Verghese Kurien
c) Dhirubhai Ambani
d) J.R.D. Tata

12. What was unusual about the Academy Award presented to Walt Disney for *Snow White and the Seven Dwarfs*?
a) The statuette was made of pure gold.
b) It was awarded posthumously.
c) The statuette could nod at the press of a button.
d) It comprised one big Oscar statuette and seven little ones.

13. The Ramon Magsaysay Award is named after a President of which country?
a) Vietnam
b) The Philippines
c) Indonesia
d) Sri Lanka

14. Which of these is the highest prize awarded at the Cannes Film Festival?
a) The Golden Bear
b) The Palme d'Or
c) The Golden Lion
d) The Honour Globe

15. In 2001, Tirana Airport in Albania was renamed after which Nobel laureate?
a) Nelson Mandela
b) The 14th Dalai Lama
c) Amartya Sen
d) Mother Teresa

16. Who was awarded the 1957 Pulitzer Prize in Biography for his book *Profiles in Courage*?
a) Neil Armstrong

b) Edmund Hillary
c) Martin Luther King Jr.
d) John F. Kennedy

17. Who was awarded the Nobel Prize 'because of his profoundly sensitive, fresh and beautiful verse, by which, with consummate skill, he has made his poetic thought, expressed in his own English words, a part of the literature of the West'?
a) Rudyard Kipling
b) Nelson Mandela
c) Ernest Hemingway
d) Rabindranath Tagore

18. The Bronze Wolf is the only award presented by . . .
a) The World Scout Committee
b) Lions Clubs International
c) The International Red Cross and Red Crescent Movement
d) World Wildlife Fund (WWF)

19. Which is the highest peacetime gallantry award in India?
a) The Padma Vibhushan
b) The Shaurya Chakra
c) The Ashok Chakra
d) The Param Vir Chakra

20. Who was the first Indian to receive both the Nobel Prize and the Bharat Ratna?
a) Amartya Sen
b) C.V. Raman
c) Mother Teresa
d) Rabindranath Tagore

CARTOONS AND COMICS

1. In the Chacha Chaudhary comics, who is the friendly alien?
   a) Sabu
   b) Kalia
   c) Rocket
   d) Billoo

2. Yogi Bear and Boo Boo live in …
   a) Jamstone National Park
   b) Picnicstone National Park
   c) Jellystone National Park
   d) Bloodstone National Park

3. In the Asterix comics, who falls into a pot of magic potion when he is a little boy?
   a) Asterix
   b) Obelix

c) Getafix
d) Vitalstatistix

4. Which comic-strip character is the personal safety mascot of NASA astronauts?
   a) Snoopy
   b) Winnie the Pooh
   c) Tweety
   d) Garfield

5. How are Huey, Dewey and Louie related to Donald Duck?
   a) They are his uncles.
   b) They are his nephews.
   c) They are his cousins.
   d) They are his brothers.

6. Jerry Siegel and Joe Shuster are the creators of which of these comic-book superheroes?
   a) Captain America
   b) Wonder Woman
   c) Batman
   d) Superman

7. Who has friends named Big Ears and Mr Plod?
   a) Noddy
   b) Winnie the Pooh
   c) Peter Pan
   d) Tintin

8. What is the name of Richie Rich's robot maid?
   a) Irona

b) Iris
c) Iridium
d) Indium

9. Which fictional character's parents are killed by Joe 'Chill' Chilton?
   a) Bruce Wayne
   b) Barry Allen
   c) Arthur Curry
   d) Victor Stone

10. What kind of creature is Spike in the cartoon series Tom and Jerry?
    a) Mouse
    b) Dog
    c) Squirrel
    d) Canary

11. Which superhero's relative says, 'With great power comes great responsibility'?
    a) Batman
    b) Superman
    c) Spiderman
    d) Green Lantern

12. With which cartoonist would you associate the *You Said It* series?
    a) R.K. Laxman
    b) Abu Abraham
    c) Mario Miranda
    d) K. Shankar Pillai

13. In the comics, Lothar is the best friend and crime-fighting companion of . . .
a) The Phantom
b) Flash Gordon
c) Mandrake
d) Jedda Walker

14. In 1937, whose statue was erected in Crystal City, Texas, to celebrate the boost in the region's spinach-growing industry?
a) Henry
b) Tintin
c) Popeye
d) Dennis the Menace

15. Who made his official film debut on 18 November 1928 in the film *Steamboat Willie*?
a) Garfield
b) Mickey Mouse
c) Donald Duck
d) Snoopy

16. Who was placed in a rocket bound for earth by his scientist parents, Jor-El and Lara?
a) Spiderman
b) Superman
c) Batman
d) Green Lantern

17. The fifth ancestor of which comic-strip character crossed swords with the pirate Blackbeard in the early 1600s?
a) Batman

b) The Phantom
c) Spiderman
d) Superman

18. Which creature does Garfield hate the most?
a) Spider
b) Ant
c) Cockroach
d) Cricket

19. In the Archie comics, who is also known as 'carrot top'?
a) Archie
b) Jughead
c) Veronica
d) Sabrina

20. In *Dennis the Menace*, what was Mr Wilson's profession before he retired?
a) Postman
b) Banker
c) Chef
d) Hairdresser

CHEMISTRY

1. In the eighteenth century, the rarity of which metal made King Louis XV of France declare it the only metal fit for a king?
   a) Tin
   b) Silver
   c) Gold
   d) Platinum

2. Why is ethyl mercaptan added to LPG that is used in kitchens?
   a) It is used as a stenching agent to detect leaks.
   b) It prevents combustion.
   c) It reduces the toxicity of LPG.
   d) It reduces the density of LPG.

3. Who gave his name to a heating device commonly used in chemistry labs?
   a) Julius Richard Petri
   b) Robert Bunsen

c) Humphry Davy
d) Carl Wilhelm Scheele

4. In the early 1900s, scientists regarded which discovery as the greatest event in chemistry since the discovery of oxygen?
a) Radium
b) X-rays
c) Raman Rays
d) Laughing gas

5. Which of these is generally used to sterilize drinking water and purify swimming pools?
a) Iodine
b) Chlorine
c) Potassium
d) Sulphur

6. Name the hardest known naturally occurring substance.
a) Pearl
b) Ruby
c) Diamond
d) Coal

7. Iridium was named after . . .
a) Ireland
b) The Latin word for 'rainbow'
c) The author Iris Murdoch
d) The flower iris

8. By what name is acetylsalicylic acid better known?
   a) Rock salt
   b) Aspirin
   c) Quicklime
   d) Vinegar

9. What did Van Helmont describe as 'something which cannot be confined in a vessel nor reduced to a visible body'?
   a) Petroleum
   b) Gas
   c) Mercury
   d) Water

10. Which metal was called 'the metal of Cyprus', as its Roman supply came almost entirely from Cyprus?
   a) Cobalt
   b) Calcium
   c) Chromium
   d) Copper

11. Helium, neon, argon, krypton and xenon are all . . .
   a) Rare earth elements
   b) Alkaline metals
   c) Inert gases
   d) Halogens

12. What is the household term for acetic acid?
   a) Turpentine oil
   b) Soya sauce
   c) Phenyl
   d) Vinegar

13. Which element forms more compounds than all the other elements combined?
a) Aluminium
b) Oxygen
c) Carbon
d) Iron

14. Quicklime is another name for . . .
a) Calcium oxide
b) Sodium chloride
c) Sulphuric acid
d) Ammonium nitrate

15. Traditionally, bronze is composed of copper and . . .
a) Carbon
b) Aluminium
c) Zinc
d) Tin

16. Which gas gives Uranus its blue tint?
a) Methane
b) Helium
c) Carbon monoxide
d) Chlorine

17. In 1806, which typist's time-saver was patented by Ralph Wedgwood?
a) Carbon paper
b) Litmus paper
c) Marble paper
d) Blotting paper

18. Which of these is called 'the universal solvent'?
   a) Petroleum
   b) Brine
   c) Water
   d) Acetic acid

19. Which is the most plentiful element in the earth's atmosphere?
   a) Ozone
   b) Neon
   c) Carbon dioxide
   d) Nitrogen

20. Name the first element to be discovered by radiochemical analysis.
   a) Uranium
   b) Radium
   c) Polonium
   d) Chromium

CHILDREN'S FILMS

1. Pongo, Perdita, Roger Radcliffe and Anita Radcliffe are some of the characters from . . .
   a) *101 Dalmatians*
   b) *Ice Age*
   c) *Madagascar*
   d) *Garfield: The Movie*

2. Which 1992 animated film had the tagline 'Imagine if you had three wishes, three hopes, three dreams and they all could come true'?
   a) *Jumanji*
   b) *Peter Pan*
   c) *Aladdin*
   d) *Sinbad: Legend of the Seven Seas*

3. In the film *The Lion King*, Simba was a lion. What kind of creature was Timon?

a) Baboon
b) Warthog
c) Hyena
d) Meerkat

4. Who played the role of Mary Poppins in the 1964 film of the same name?

a) Julie Andrews
b) Katharine Hepburn
c) Vivien Leigh
d) Ginger Rogers

5. What type of extinct animal was Diego in the 2002 film *Ice Age*?

a) Saber-toothed tiger
b) Mammoth
c) Ground sloth
d) Quagga

6. *Krrish* is the sequel to which Bollywood blockbuster?

a) *Koi Mil Gaya*
b) *Makdee*
c) *Jajantaram Mamantaram*
d) *Jo Jeeta Wohi Sikandar*

7. One of the tag lines of which of these films is 'It ain't the Cat in the Hat'?

a) *Garfield*
b) *Chicken Little*

c) *Madagascar*
d) *Puss in Boots*

8. If a killer whale is the titular character in the film *Free Willy*, then what is the titular animal in the film *Flipper*?
   a) A clownfish
   b) A dolphin
   c) A shark
   d) A duck

9. Which was India's first 3D film?
   a) *My Dear Kuttichathan*
   b) *Roadside Romeo*
   c) *Ra.One*
   d) *Bal Ganesh*

10. What is the name of Troy Bolton's basketball team in the film *High School Musical*?
    a) Wildcats
    b) Crazy Bears
    c) Black Panthers
    d) Green Goblins

11. Apart from Victor and Laverne, who is Quasimodo's gargoyle friend in the Walt Disney film *The Hunchback of Notre Dame*?
    a) Hugo
    b) Frollo
    c) Clopin
    d) Phoebus

12. Which was the first animated Disney film based on historical facts?
   a) *Snow White and the Seven Dwarfs*
   b) *Sleeping Beauty*
   c) *Pocahontas*
   d) *The Little Mermaid*

13. In the film *Stanley ka Dabba*, what is the 'dabba'?
   a) A pencil box
   b) A piggy bank
   c) A tiffin box
   d) A suitcase

14. What is the name of the park that the character called John Hammond builds on Isla Nublar, off the Costa Rican coast?
   a) Jellystone Park
   b) Wonderland
   c) Jurassic Park
   d) Westworld

15. According to the Guinness World Records, which was the first feature-length computer-animated film?
   a) *Shrek*
   b) *Ice Age*
   c) *Toy Story*
   d) *Frozen*

16. They were born as Arthur Stanley and Oliver Norvell. A famous pair, how are they better known?
   a) Bonnie and Clyde
   b) Laurel and Hardy

c) Tom and Jerry
d) The Marx Brothers

17. In which film would you meet these seven children—Liesl, Louisa, Friedrich, Kurt, Brigitta, Marta and Gretl?
    a) *Mrs Doubtfire*
    b) *Willy Wonka and the Chocolate Factory*
    c) *The Sound of Music*
    d) *The Wizard of Oz*

18. The 2003 animated film *Finding Nemo* features which geographical location?
    a) Antarctica
    b) The Great Barrier Reef
    c) The Himalayas
    d) The Amazon rainforest

19. In the film *Makdee*, what does the witch turn Munni into?
    a) A balloon
    b) A hen
    c) A statue
    d) A rose

20. *The Blue Umbrella* is based on a novella by . . .
    a) R.K. Narayan
    b) Ruskin Bond
    c) Rudyard Kipling
    d) Mulk Raj Anand

CHILDREN'S LITERATURE

1. Which fictional character has stepsisters named Anastasia and Drizella?
   a) Sleeping Beauty
   b) Snow White
   c) Goldilocks
   d) Cinderella

2. Name Tinker Bell's friend who never grows up.
   a) Tom Sawyer
   b) Harry Potter
   c) Peter Pan
   d) Jim Hawkins

3. Alexander Selkirk, a Scottish sailor, provided the inspiration for which story?
   a) *Twenty Thousand Leagues under the Sea*
   b) *Moby Dick*

c) *Treasure Island*
d) *Robinson Crusoe*

4. Whose autobiography is called *The Fairy Tale of My Life*?
   a) Hans Christian Andersen
   b) Charles Dickens
   c) J.M. Barrie
   d) Carlo Collodi

5. 'Yours is the Earth and everything that's in it. And—which is more—you'll be a Man, my son!' These are the last few lines of which poem?
   a) 'The Charge of the Light Brigade'
   b) 'Lochinvar'
   c) 'If'
   d) 'Where the Mind Is Without Fear'

6. According to a novel by Alexandre Dumas, how is Edmond Dantes better known?
   a) The Hunchback of Notre Dame
   b) The Count of Monte Cristo
   c) The Wonderful Wizard of Oz
   d) The Hobbit

7. In which work would you come across Chingachgook and his son, Uncas?
   a) *The Last of the Mohicans*
   b) *The Call of the Wild*
   c) *Charlie and the Chocolate Factory*
   d) *Kidnapped*

8. Which book, published in 1852, was smuggled into Russia in Yiddish to evade Czarist censors?
   a) *Gulliver's Travels*
   b) *Black Beauty*
   c) *Alice's Adventures in Wonderland*
   d) *Uncle Tom's Cabin*

9. Which famous novel begins with the words 'Call me Ishmael'?
   a) *Peter Pan*
   b) *1984*
   c) *Moby Dick*
   d) *The Time Machine*

10. Which children's novel by Dodie Smith is also a Walt Disney film?
   a) *The Little Mermaid*
   b) *The Lion King*
   c) *The Hundred and One Dalmatians*
   d) *Pocahontas*

11. Which popular story was originally titled *The Sea Cook*?
   a) *Treasure Island*
   b) *The Old Man and the Sea*
   c) *Around the World in Eighty Days*
   d) *Moby Dick*

12. In *Twenty Thousand Leagues under the Sea*, what is the name of the warship in which Captain Nemo sails?
   a) *Nautilus*
   b) *Aurora*

   c) *Jolly Roger*
   d) *Pequod*

13. Charles Dickens is said to have based the character of Mr Micawber on ...
   a) Himself
   b) His father
   c) His friend Edgar Allan Poe
   d) His teacher

14. Victor Hugo wrote a novel about a fifteenth-century bell-ringer, Quasimodo, who suffers from a physical deformity. Identify the novel.
   a) *The Swiss Family Robinson*
   b) *The Count of Monte Cristo*
   c) *The Wonderful Wizard of Oz*
   d) *The Hunchback of Notre Dame*

15. In 1865, the first edition of which book by an English mathematician was withdrawn because of bad printing?
   a) *A Tale of Two Cities*
   b) *Alice's Adventures in Wonderland*
   c) *A Christmas Carol*
   d) *A Journey to the Center of the Earth*

16. In 'Jack and the Beanstalk', what is Milky White?
   a) The name of the bean he had planted
   b) The house in which Jack lived
   c) The name of the cow that Jack traded for some beans
   d) The river behind Jack's house

17. What is the name of the she-wolf who suckles Mowgli?
   a) Raksha
   b) Sandhya
   c) Kaa
   d) Maya

18. Who created the characters Parvati and Padma Patil?
   a) Eoin Colfer
   b) Stephenie Meyer
   c) J.K. Rowling
   d) Suzanne Collins

19. In the nursery rhyme, what does Little Bo-Peep lose?
   a) Cat
   b) Dog
   c) Sheep
   d) Horse

20. Whose cradle is a walnut shell?
   a) Rapunzel
   b) Sleeping Beauty
   c) Thumbelina
   d) Snow White

CLOTHES AND ACCESSORIES

1. Which of these garments is secured at the waist by a broad sash known as an obi?
   a) Kimono
   b) Kilt
   c) Poncho
   d) Kaftan

2. In medieval times, a knight threw down a gauntlet to challenge someone to a duel. Which part of his attire was a gauntlet?
   a) The plume of his helmet
   b) His glove
   c) His broadsword
   d) His signet ring

3. Where might you meet Nishi warriors, wearing hornbill feathers in their caps and carrying knives in monkey-skin scabbards?
   a) Jharkhand

b) Madhya Pradesh
c) Chhattisgarh
d) Arunachal Pradesh

4. A cylindrical canvas bag closed by a drawstring and carried over the shoulder is known as a ...
   a) Portmanteau
   b) Duffel bag
   c) Attache case
   d) Tote bag

5. In 1848, uniforms made of which fabric were introduced by Sir H.B. Lumsden and W. Hodson for British colonial troops in India?
   a) Rayon
   b) Flannel
   c) Denim
   d) Khaki

6. Which of these saris is traditionally from Gujarat?
   a) Patola
   b) Paithani
   c) Maheshwari
   d) Chanderi

7. In India, which intricate shadow-work embroidery uses white yarn on colourless muslin called *tanzeb*?
   a) Kantha
   b) Chikankari
   c) Phulkari
   d) Kalamkari

8. Which practice was first recorded by James Cook during his expedition to Tahiti in 1769?
a) Tattooing
b) Henna application
c) Hair dyeing
d) Nose piercing

9. Why were copper rivets put on denim jeans?
a) They did not allow the material to sag.
b) They prevented creases.
c) They were just part of the design.
d) They prevented the pockets from tearing under the weight of tools and increased their durability.

10. On which part of the body are mittens worn?
a) Waist
b) Ankle
c) Hands
d) Head

11. In which present-day state of India did calico, a type of cotton cloth, originate?
a) Rajasthan
b) Assam
c) Andhra Pradesh
d) Kerala

12. What are 'bowler' and 'sombrero' types of?
a) Hats
b) Skirts

c) Trousers

d) Shoes

13. Which of these is a long coat worn by men in India?

a) Mekhala

b) Achkan

c) Uttariya

d) Dhoti

14. Which accessory could you buy using the measuring instrument Brannock Device?

a) Ring

b) Shoes

c) Necktie

d) Hat

15. On which part of your body would you wear a kippah?

a) Head

b) Feet

c) Wrist

d) Ears

16. Traditionally, the men of which country wear a *gho*?

a) Bhutan

b) Sri Lanka

c) Thailand

d) Indonesia

17. What came into use in the seventeenth century after Louis XIII began wearing one in 1624?

a) Perukes, or men's wigs

b) Tattoos

c) Cummerbunds, or sashes worn around the waist

d) Jodhpurs, or trousers meant for horse riding

18. A pair of Bermudas will reach your . . .

a) Knees

b) Thighs

c) Ankles

d) Calves

19. The plain-woven cotton fabric known as muslin is named after the city of Mosul. In which country is Mosul located?

a) Iraq

b) Iran

c) Saudi Arabia

d) Turkey

20. Tassar, Eri and Muga are varieties of which fabric?

a) Silk

b) Jute

c) Cotton

d) Linen

COMPUTERS AND
THE INTERNET

1. In 1963, Douglas Engelbart created the first working model of a device. Twenty years later, what was mass-produced using his idea?
   a) Printer
   b) Computer mouse
   c) CD
   d) Monitor

2. In the binary system, which two digits represent all numbers?
   a) Zero and one
   b) One and two
   c) Five and six
   d) Zero and nine

3. Which computer language shares its name with the fourth-largest island of Indonesia?
a) Cobol
b) Java
c) Algol
d) Pascal

4. Ray Tomlinson is credited with . . .
a) Sending the first email
b) Writing the first computer virus
c) Developing the computer language Pascal
d) Designing the computer mouse

5. In computing, what is a nibble?
a) It is a cell in an Excel sheet.
b) It is a special code used in URLs.
c) It is half a byte.
d) It is an output language.

6. Which of these is a programme designed to breach security in the guise of performing some harmless function?
a) Adobe Photoshop
b) OpenOffice
c) Malwarebytes
d) Trojan horse

7. Which of these phrases first appeared in a 1987 article in *Whole Earth Review*?
a) Virtual community
b) Cybercrime

c) Internet crawling

d) Home page

8. On a Windows computer, what is pressed along with the Ctrl key to display the Start menu?

a) Shift

b) Enter

c) Esc

d) Tab

9. Who is credited with having conceived the first automatic digital computer?

a) Ada Lovelace

b) Blaise Pascal

c) Grace Hopper

d) Charles Babbage

10. '.es' is the Internet country code of ...

a) Eritrea

b) Spain

c) Italy

d) Estonia

11. What name was chosen by its inventor over the names Mesh and The Information Mine?

a) Laptop

b) Malware

c) Mouse

d) World Wide Web

12. In computing, what are Garamond, Century and Verdana different types of?
a) Fonts
b) Computer languages
c) Drawing tools
d) Alignment techniques

13. In computer technology, what is wetware?
a) The human brain
b) A freshly printed page
c) The best swimsuit catalogue on the Net
d) An ink cartridge for a bubble jet printer

14. On a computer keyboard, if the Ctrl key stands for 'control', what does the Alt key stand for?
a) Alternate
b) Alignment
c) Answer
d) Allow

15. If RAM stands for Random Access Memory, what does ROM stand for?
a) Read-Only Memory
b) Real-Output Memory
c) Refer-Outline Memory
d) Reset-Only Memory

16. The word 'pixel' is an abbreviation of 'picture' and ...
a) Elasticity
b) Element

c) Exit

d) Electronics

17. Which of these is an input device?
   a) Printer
   b) Keyboard
   c) Monitor
   d) Speaker

18. In computing, the full form of WORM is Write Once Read ...
   a) More
   b) Many
   c) Minute
   d) Multiple

19. Where might you come across a trackball?
   a) Hard drive
   b) Mouse
   c) Monitor
   d) Motherboard

20. Ada Lovelace, often called the first computer programmer, was the daughter of which famous poet?
   a) Lord Byron
   b) William Wordsworth
   c) P.B. Shelley
   d) John Keats

CRICKET

1. What is the postbox number of the Australian Broadcasting Corporation, created as a tribute to Don Bradman's Test batting average?
   a) 9990
   b) 9991
   c) 9994
   d) 9999

2. A yorker is a delivery that is pitched between the bat and the legs of a batsman. How did it get its name?
   a) It is a concept adapted from the New York Giants.
   b) The commentator who named the first delivery was from York.
   c) The umpires of that match ate egg yolks for breakfast.
   d) It was introduced by players from Yorkshire.

3. What is the nickname of the New Zealand cricket team?
   a) Black Caps
   b) Black Bats
   c) Black Hats
   d) All Blacks

4. Who was the first batsman in the history of international cricket to be given out by the third umpire?
   a) Brian Lara
   b) Sachin Tendulkar
   c) Kumar Sangakkara
   d) Ricky Ponting

5. Which cricket stadium is named after Lord Auckland's sisters?
   a) Adelaide Oval
   b) The Wanderers
   c) Old Trafford
   d) Eden Gardens

6. Against which team did the Indian women's cricket team play its first Test match?
   a) England
   b) West Indies
   c) New Zealand
   d) Australia

7. The Bombay Pentangular was a . . .
   a) Pre-Duckworth-Lewis method
   b) Pre-Independence tournament
   c) Trophy that was replaced by the urn in the Ashes series
   d) Type of extra that is now discontinued

8. Which English cricketer, who's also a doctor, was known for treating his poorer patients without charging a fee?
  a) Wally Hammond
  b) Len Hutton
  c) W.G. Grace
  d) Jack Hobbs

9. Which term owes its origins to a mock obituary of English cricket in the *Sporting Times*?
  a) Doosra
  b) Ashes
  c) Chinaman
  d) Googly

10. Whose father has also played ODIs for India?
  a) M.S. Dhoni
  b) Yuvraj Singh
  c) Virender Sehwag
  d) Manish Pandey

11. In cricketing slang, what is sometimes referred to as a 'brain bucket'?
  a) The baggy green cap
  b) A helmet
  c) A delivery that hits the batsman on the head
  d) A wicketkeeper with one glove

12. Which continent has the most number of Test-playing nations?
  a) Europe
  b) Africa

c) Asia
d) South America

13. A 'Rest of the World vs MCC' match played at Lord's in 1987 was which Indian cricketer's last first-class match?
a) Kapil Dev
b) Ravi Shastri
c) Sunil Gavaskar
d) Gundappa Viswanath

14. If you are standing at the 'long stop' position in cricket, where would your fielding position be?
a) At the boundary, directly behind the umpire
b) At the boundary, directly behind the wicketkeeper
c) At first slip
d) At silly point

15. In cricket, which is the least common form of dismissal?
a) Timed out
b) Handling the ball
c) Leg before wicket
d) Obstructing the field

16. How is Maharaja Jam Saheb of Nawanagar better known to us?
a) Mansur Ali Khan
b) K.S. Ranjitsinhji
c) Yuvraj Singh
d) Ajay Jadeja

17. Ajinkya Rahane holds the record for being the last person to do what in international cricket?
a) Bowl with two hands
b) Wear a chest guard
c) Be a runner
d) Be captain in his debut Test

18. To what did spin bowler Bishan Singh Bedi attribute his strong and supple fingers?
a) His suffering from polio as a child
b) His piano lessons
c) Him being a champion marble player as a child
d) Helping his mother make lassi

19. When a cricket umpire touches both shoulders with his hands crossed in front of him, what is he signalling?
a) Change of decision
b) One run short
c) Dead ball
d) There is no such signal.

20. Which of the following terms is used for the doctoring of the ball at the seam to give it unnatural movement?
a) Slogging
b) Sledging
c) Scuffing
d) Battering

DISEASES AND DISORDERS

1. What important role did James Phipps play in the history of medicine?
   a) He invented the pacemaker.
   b) He was the first blood donor.
   c) He underwent the first open-heart surgery.
   d) He was given the first vaccination against smallpox by Edward Jenner.

2. A stroke is caused by the interruption of blood supply to the ...
   a) Lungs
   b) Brain
   c) Kidneys
   d) Heart

3. Alopecia areata is a common skin disease, causing ...
   a) Hair loss
   b) Black patches

c) Rashes
d) Wrinkles

4. Which gland swells to a goitre?
   a) Adrenal gland
   b) Pituitary gland
   c) Thyroid gland
   d) Parotid gland

5. Which of these diseases is caused by the varicella virus?
   a) Chickenpox
   b) Leprosy
   c) Pertussis
   d) Rabies

6. An odontologist deals with the structure and diseases of the ...
   a) Ears
   b) Heart
   c) Teeth
   d) Kidneys

7. Which two colours are mixed up in the most common type of colour blindness?
   a) Red and green
   b) Blue and yellow
   c) Red and blue
   d) White and black

8. If you had excess bilirubin in your bloodstream, what would you be suffering from?
   a) Meningitis
   b) Measles
   c) Glaucoma
   d) Jaundice

9. Encephalitis is a disease that affects the brain. Which part of your body is affected when you have hepatitis?
   a) Heart
   b) Brain
   c) Liver
   d) Lungs

10. Which of these is thought to be the most common cause of anaemia globally?
   a) Iron deficiency
   b) Parasitic infections
   c) Vitamin K deficiency
   d) Diabetes

11. In human beings, which was the first organ to be transplanted successfully?
   a) Kidney
   b) Heart
   c) Cornea
   d) Liver

12. Which part of the body does pneumonia mainly affect?
   a) Bones
   b) Lungs

c) Brain

d) Stomach

13. Malaria is caused by . . .
    a) The bite of female anopheles mosquitoes
    b) Drinking contaminated water
    c) An airborne virus
    d) The bite of a mad dog

14. Which of these is a mild form of seborrhoeic dermatitis that affects the scalp?
    a) Ringworm
    b) Dandruff
    c) Folliculitis
    d) Psoriasis

15. Scurvy is caused due to a deficiency of which vitamin in the human body?
    a) Vitamin K
    b) Vitamin C
    c) Vitamin D
    d) Vitamin B1

16. Which of these oils is used as a local anaesthetic for toothaches?
    a) Mustard oil
    b) Clove oil
    c) Olive oil
    d) Coconut oil

17. If you suffered from halitosis, what would you be suffering from?
a) Bad breath
b) Baldness
c) Short-sightedness
d) Sleeplessness

18. Which of these is a non-communicable disease?
a) Pertussis
b) Ebola
c) Influenza
d) Diabetes

19. In 1980, the World Health Organization declared the world free of . . .
a) Smallpox
b) Polio
c) Tuberculosis
d) Diphtheria

20. Which of these terms is derived from the Greek words meaning 'half of the head'?
a) Agnosia
b) Encephalitis
c) Migraine
d) Meningitis

FAMOUS WOMEN

1. According to UNESCO, who is the most translated woman author in the world?
   a) Enid Blyton
   b) Charlotte Brontë
   c) Jane Austen
   d) Agatha Christie

2. Who was Anne Sullivan's famous deaf and blind pupil?
   a) Louis Braille
   b) Helen Keller
   c) Ray Charles
   d) Thomas Alva Edison

3. Who was queen of the United Kingdom of Great Britain and Ireland (1837–1901) and empress of India (1876–1901)?
   a) Queen Victoria
   b) Mary, Queen of Scots

c) Queen Elizabeth II
d) Queen Anne

4. Who among these coined the term 'radioactivity'?
a) Grace Hopper
b) Marie Curie
c) Irene Joliot-Curie
d) Gerty Cori

5. Who played the titular role in the 1945 Tamil film *Meera*?
a) M.S. Subbulakshmi
b) Kishori Amonkar
c) Girija Devi
d) Gangubai Hangal

6. Sirimavo Bandaranaike was the first woman in the world to . . .
a) Become prime minister of a country
b) Receive an Oscar in the Best Supporting Actor category
c) Win the Ramon Magsaysay Award
d) Reach the summit of Mount Everest

7. This famous lady was born on 6 March 1937 in Russia. She became a member of the Supreme Soviet in 1966. Name her.
a) Sally Ride
b) Valentina Tereshkova
c) Valery Bykovsky
d) Svetlana Savitskaya

8. In 1953, whose notes were reintroduced in *Faster Than Thought: A Symposium on Digital Computing Machines*?
a) Florence Nightingale

b) Edith Clarke
c) Ada Lovelace
d) Grace Hopper

9. Jane Goodall was famous for her long-term research on which animal at the Gombe Stream National Park, Tanzania?
   a) Elephants
   b) Chimpanzees
   c) Pythons
   d) Lions

10. Meryl Streep played the role of which politician in the film *The Iron Lady*?
    a) Margaret Thatcher
    b) Angela Merkel
    c) Theresa May
    d) Hillary Clinton

11. In 1952, who established Nirmal Hriday, a hospice for the terminally ill?
    a) Annie Besant
    b) The Mother
    c) Mother Teresa
    d) Sister Nivedita

12. In 1972, who became the first woman to join the Indian Police Service?
    a) Kiran Bedi
    b) Bachendri Pal
    c) M. Fathima Beevi
    d) Chhavi Rajawat

13. Who among these women helped form The Ninety-Nines, an international organization for the advancement of female pilots?
a) Amelia Earhart
b) Valentina Tereshkova
c) Amy Johnson
d) Harriet Quimby

14. Who was the international president of the Theosophical Society from 1907 until her death?
a) Annie Besant
b) Rukmini Devi Arundale
c) Sarojini Naidu
d) Sister Nivedita

15. *Notes on _____: What It Is and What It Is Not.* Fill in the blank to complete the name of this book by Florence Nightingale.
a) *Cleanliness*
b) *Statistics*
c) *Nursing*
d) *Health*

16. Who was the first woman president of the United Nations General Assembly?
a) Nandini Satpathy
b) Sucheta Kripalini
c) Sarojini Naidu
d) Vijaya Lakshmi Pandit

17. On which planet would you find Chawla Hill, named after Kalpana Chawla?
a) Mercury
b) Venus
c) Mars
d) Jupiter

18. Who won the Nobel Prize 'for her non-violent struggle for democracy and human rights'?
a) Mother Teresa
b) Shirin Ebadi
c) Doris Lessing
d) Aung San Suu Kyi

19. Which former prime minister wrote an autobiography titled *Daughter of the East*?
a) Benazir Bhutto
b) Sheikh Hasina
c) Indira Gandhi
d) Chandrika Kumaratunga

20. During which war did Joan of Arc lead the French army?
a) The Hundred Years' War
b) The French Revolution
c) World War II
d) The Crimean War

FICTION

1. In *Gulliver's Travels*, what causes the war between Lilliput and its neighbour?
   a) The gold on Gulliver's ship
   b) A land dispute
   c) A dispute over whether to eat soup or drink soup
   d) A dispute over whether to break the broad or narrow end of an egg

2. Which novel ends with the words 'God bless us, every one!'?
   a) *David Copperfield*
   b) *A Christmas Carol*
   c) *Oliver Twist*
   d) *Barnaby Rudge*

3. What is the name of Harry Potter's pet owl?
   a) Kreacher
   b) Hokey

c) Hedwig

d) Nagini

4. Which author said that her goal in writing her only novel was 'to induce kindness, sympathy and an understanding treatment of horses'?

   a) Johanna Spyri

   b) Beatrix Potter

   c) Anna Sewell

   d) Jane Austen

5. For how many years did Rip Van Winkle sleep?

   a) Five years

   b) Ten years

   c) Twenty years

   d) Fifty years

6. My friend lives in Mapleton and I have a housekeeper named Hannah Gruen. Who am I?

   a) Miss Marple

   b) Heidi

   c) Nancy Drew

   d) Sherlock Holmes

7. In which fictional town would you find Albert Mission College, Lawley Extension and Mempi Hills?

   a) Malgudi

   b) Wessex

   c) Emerald City

   d) Hogsmeade

8. In literature, A.A. Milne is well known for creating popular stories about Christopher Robin and Winnie the Pooh. Winnie the Pooh is a toy...
   a) Kangaroo
   b) Bear
   c) Wolf
   d) Tiger

9. In the book *The Adventures of Tom Sawyer*, how does the villain, Injun Joe, die?
   a) A chicken bone gets stuck in his throat.
   b) He drowns in a lake.
   c) He is trapped in a cave and dies of starvation.
   d) Tom forces him to swallow a cricket.

10. In Jane Austen's novel *Pride and Prejudice*, Mr and Mrs Bennet have five daughters: Jane, Elizabeth, Mary, Lydia and...
    a) Mili
    b) Annie
    c) Kitty
    d) Liz

11. Which fictional boy fell out of his carriage and was taken by fairies to Never Never Land?
    a) Noddy
    b) Tom Sawyer
    c) Harry Potter
    d) Peter Pan

12. In which of these books would you come across the phrase 'Four legs good, two legs bad'?
   a) *Black Beauty*
   b) *Animal Farm*
   c) *The Jungle Book*
   d) *Born Free*

13. Who is assisted by a group of fellow outlaws known as the Merry Men?
   a) James Bond
   b) Harry Potter
   c) Sherlock Holmes
   d) Robin Hood

14. In the fairy tale, who eats baby bear's porridge, breaks his chair and sleeps in his bed?
   a) Rapunzel
   b) Cinderella
   c) Sleeping Beauty
   d) Goldilocks

15. In the Secret Seven books, what is the name of Peter and Janet's golden spaniel?
   a) Scamper
   b) Montmorency
   c) Snowy
   d) Toto

16. Which novel did D.H. Lawrence describe as 'An epic of the sea such as no man has equalled'?
   a) *Treasure Island*

b) *Moby Dick*

c) *Robinson Crusoe*

d) *The Old Man and the Sea*

17. Which literary character's favourite phrase is 'Off with his head!'?

a) King Lear

b) Quasimodo

c) Captain Hook

d) The Queen of Hearts

18. Cinderella got her name because she . . .

a) Loved eating cinnamon cakes

b) Sat in the chimney corner, among cinders, after work

c) Was born in Cincinnati

d) Had a brother named Cinderfella

19. Which collection of stories is also called *Alf Laylah Wa Laylah*?

a) *Arabian Nights*

b) The Jataka Tales

c) *Panchatantra*

d) *Hitopadesha*

20. In Rudyard Kipling's *The Jungle Book*, what kind of creature is Baloo?

a) Brown bear

b) Snake

c) Monkey

d) Hedgehog

FREEDOM STRUGGLE OF INDIA

1. Who said, 'Every blow aimed at me is a nail in the coffin of British imperialism'?
   a) Abul Kalam Azad
   b) Bipin Chandra Pal
   c) Lala Lajpat Rai
   d) Lal Bahadur Shastri

2. In 1930, who started the Vanar Sena, a children's brigade to help freedom fighters?
   a) Bhagat Singh
   b) Khudiram Bose
   c) Vijaya Lakshmi Pandit
   d) Indira Gandhi

3. In which present-day state did the Kakori train robbery take place?
   a) West Bengal
   b) Madhya Pradesh
   c) Bihar
   d) Uttar Pradesh

4. Which Indian freedom fighter and social reformer transformed Ganesha Chaturthi into a public event in Maharashtra?
   a) Lokmanya Tilak
   b) Lala Lajpat Rai
   c) Mahadev Govind Ranade
   d) Bipin Chandra Pal

5. On what grounds was Surendranath Banerjee's admission to the Indian Civil Service (now IAS) rejected?
   a) He misrepresented his age.
   b) His IQ was below fifty-five.
   c) He wrote the words 'surrender not' instead of Surendranath.
   d) Only women were allowed in the ICS.

6. 'The saint has left our shores, I hope, forever,' wrote a statesman named Smuts. Who was the saint?
   a) Jawaharlal Nehru
   b) Mahatma Gandhi
   c) Dadabhai Naoroji
   d) Bal Gangadhar Tilak

7. With which two words did Jawaharlal Nehru conclude his 'Tryst with Destiny' speech?
a) 'Satyameva jayate'
b) 'Jai Hind'
c) 'Vande mataram'
d) 'Inquilab zindabad'

8. Who led the fifteen-day Salt Satyagraha march in Tamil Nadu, from Trichy to Vedaranyam, in 1930?
a) T.T. Krishnamachari
b) S. Radhakrishnan
c) C. Rajagopalachari
d) K. Kamaraj

9. The slogan *'Karenge ya marenge'* ('Do or die') was coined for which famous movement in India?
a) Khilafat Movement
b) Quit India Movement
c) Civil Disobedience Movement
d) Formation of the Azad Hind Fauj

10. Which leader was also known as Frontier Gandhi?
a) Vallabhbhai Patel
b) Lala Lajpat Rai
c) Bal Gangadhar Tilak
d) Abdul Ghaffar Khan

11. The role of which freedom fighter was played by Aamir Khan in a 2005 film directed by Ketan Mehta?
a) Bhagat Singh
b) Mangal Pandey

c) Chandrasekhar Azad
d) Khudiram Bose

12. Which leader wrote *Srimad Bhagavad Gita Rahasya* while he was jailed in Myanmar?
a) Bal Gangadhar Tilak
b) Motilal Nehru
c) Gopal Krishna Gokhale
d) Dadabhai Naoroji

13. In 1929, who was elected president of the Lahore session of the Indian National Congress, where complete independence for the country was adopted as the goal?
a) Jawaharlal Nehru
b) Vallabhbhai Patel
c) Abul Kalam Azad
d) Bal Gangadhar Tilak

14. Who made his escape disguised as Md Ziauddin, an insurance agent?
a) Vallabhbhai Patel
b) Jawaharlal Nehru
c) Mahatma Gandhi
d) Subhas Chandra Bose

15. In 1906, which word was coined after Maganlal Gandhi replied to a contest in the South African journal *Indian Opinion*?
a) Ahimsa
b) Satyagraha

c) Harijan
d) Dalit

16. In his *Poverty and Un-British Rule in India,* who stated that India's wealth was being drained away to England?
a) Dadabhai Naoroji
b) Syed Ahmed Khan
c) Abul Kalam Azad
d) Gopal Krishna Gokhale

17. Who was the first non-Indian president of the Indian National Congress?
a) William Wedderburn
b) George Yule
c) Alfred Webb
d) A.O. Hume

18. Ghadar was a movement among Indians living in North America to end British rule in India. What does the word *ghadar* mean in Urdu?
a) Victory
b) Revolution
c) Truth
d) Motherland

19. In 1922, which incident forced Gandhiji to suspend the Civil Disobedience Movement?
a) The Kakori train robbery
b) The Jallianwala Bagh massacre
c) The Chauri Chaura incident
d) The Chittagong armoury raid

20. On which occasion did Sarojini Naidu write to Jawaharlal Nehru, 'Love to all and a kiss to the new soul of India'?
   a) When India achieved independence
   b) On the birth of Indira Gandhi
   c) At the start of the Quit India Movement
   d) After he was sworn in as prime minister

GEOGRAPHICAL TERMS

1. According to belief, the horse latitudes got their name...
   a) From the surname of John Callcott Horsley
   b) From the practice of throwing horses overboard from becalmed ships to save water
   c) Because the trade winds blow at very high speeds
   d) Because crews survived on horseradish in that region

2. Crescentic, linear, star, dome and parabolic are types of...
   a) Sand dunes
   b) Clouds
   c) Constellations
   d) Caves

3. From 1979 onwards, what are named alphabetically, alternating between male and female names?
   a) Mountain peaks
   b) Hurricanes

c) Newly discovered dwarf planets
d) Newly discovered islands

4. A mass of rocks and sediment carried down and deposited by a glacier is known as . . .
a) Sleet
b) Iceberg
c) Moraine
d) Flurry

5. What do you call the lines on a map that connect places receiving the same amount of rainfall in a given period?
a) Isohel
b) Isotherm
c) Isobar
d) Isohyet

6. Which of these is a dry and dusty trade wind blowing from the north-east/easterly direction over north-west Africa?
a) Foehn
b) Chinook
c) Harmattan
d) Bora

7. Which word is the fourth letter of the Greek alphabet as well as a triangular tract of sediment deposited at the mouth of a river?
a) Gamma
b) Beta
c) Alpha
d) Delta

8. What do you call a narrow strip of land with sea on either side, joining two larger masses of land?
a) Fjord
b) Gulf
c) Cove
d) Isthmus

9. The name Antarctica means . . .
a) 'Covered with snow'
b) 'Opposite to the Arctic'
c) 'Barren land'
d) 'Remote land'

10. Which biome surrounds the North and South poles and is characterized by extremely cold climate and few plants and animals?
a) Tundra
b) Steppes
c) Savannah
d) Taiga

11. Which rocks are formed from the solidification of magma?
a) Igneous
b) Sedimentary
c) Metamorphic
d) Mudrocks

12. A detailed description or representation on a map of the physical features of an area is called . . .
a) Archaeology
b) Palaeontology

c) Topography

d) Demography

13. Connect a part of the human body with the calm region at the centre of a storm.

a) Eye

b) Heart

c) Brain

d) Navel

14. The word 'petroleum' comes from the Latin words *petra* and *oleum*. If 'oleum' means oil, then 'petra' means . . .

a) Fire

b) Gas

c) Ocean

d) Rock

15. Which of these generally forms a funnel made up of water droplets, dust and debris?

a) Tornado

b) Doldrum

c) Gyre

d) Avalanche

16. Luke Howard, a meteorologist, called the high, wispy clouds 'cirrus' as they reminded him of . . .

a) Snowflakes

b) Curls of hair

c) Candyfloss

d) Cotton fibre

17. Rain that contains a high concentration of pollutants, notably sulphur and nitrogen oxides, is known as . . .
a) Acid rain
b) Basic rain
c) Sleet
d) Hail

18. Which of these instruments is used for measuring atmospheric pressure?
a) Anemometer
b) Barometer
c) Odometer
d) Magnetometer

19. Which word stands for the large hollow forming the mouth of a volcano as well as a large bowl-shaped cavity on a celestial object?
a) Caldera
b) Crater
c) Corrie
d) Cone

20. Which of these is a column of calcium carbonate growing upwards from the floor of a cave?
a) Stalactite
b) Ore
c) Stalagmite
d) Loess

GEOGRAPHY OF INDIA

1. What did the raja of Sikkim gift the British on 1 February 1835?
   a) Mount Everest
   b) Kaziranga National Park
   c) Darjeeling
   d) The Ganges

2. Dudhsagar, Hogenakkal and Chitrakoot are names of . . .
   a) Mountain peaks
   b) Waterfalls
   c) Plateaus
   d) Lakes

3. Barren Island, of the Andaman and Nicobar Islands, has India's . . .
   a) Only active volcano
   b) Smallest freshwater lake

c) Highest waterfall
d) Largest dam

4. Till 1972, which state was called the North-East Frontier Agency and was a part of the state of Assam?
a) Arunachal Pradesh
b) Odisha
c) Sikkim
d) Nagaland

5. According to the Guinness World Records, which of these is the largest river island in the world?
a) Salsette
b) Majuli
c) Umananda
d) Havelock

6. Why did the British settle in houseboats in Kashmir?
a) To practise their favourite sport, rowing
b) They were barred from buying land.
c) To protect their daughters from mixing with the 'locals'
d) The city was too congested and dirty.

7. Of the following states, which state has the longest coastline?
a) Gujarat
b) Tamil Nadu
c) Kerala
d) Maharashtra

8. Which Indian city's former names were Pataligram, Kusumpur and Azimabad?
   a) Allahabad
   b) Kanpur
   c) Lucknow
   d) Patna

9. The zero mile marker, indicating the geographical centre of India, is located in which city?
   a) Nagpur
   b) Kanpur
   c) Cuttack
   d) Bhopal

10. Traditionally, which river forms the boundary between north India and south India?
    a) Godavari
    b) Krishna
    c) Indus
    d) Narmada

11. Though the name of this Union Territory means 'hundred thousand islands', it has only ten inhabited islands. Name it.
    a) Daman and Diu
    b) Lakshadweep
    c) Chandigarh
    d) Puducherry

12. In 1819, which of these landmarks was discovered by an army officer in the Madras Regiment during one of his hunting expeditions?
   a) The ruins of Nalanda
   b) The Ajanta Caves
   c) Naini Lake
   d) Shore Temple

13. With what would you associate the shape of the Gulf of Khambhat?
   a) A trumpet
   b) A bean
   c) A pear
   d) A hammer

14. Which present-day Indian city was given to Great Britain by Portugal as part of the dowry of Catherine of Braganza when she married Charles II?
   a) Kochi
   b) Chennai
   c) Mumbai
   d) Puducherry

15. Which month does the south-west monsoon generally arrive in Kerala?
   a) May
   b) June
   c) July
   d) August

16. Across which river is the Hirakud Dam built?
   a) Mahanadi

b) Godavari
c) Krishna
d) Kaveri

17. The Great Rann of Kutch, covering an area of about 18,000
square kilometres, lies almost entirely within which state?
a) Gujarat
b) Madhya Pradesh
c) Karnataka
d) Jammu and Kashmir

18. Which of these places has a 100-year-old extant oilfield and
the oldest operating oil refinery in the world?
a) Digboi
b) Barauni
c) Dhanbad
d) Jamnagar

19. The capital of which Indian state is named after Anantha, the
cosmic serpent with a thousand heads?
a) Karnataka
b) Kerala
c) Tamil Nadu
d) Andhra Pradesh

20. This lake was formed as a result of a meteorite crash around
50,000 years ago. It is the world's only hyper-velocity impact
crater in basaltic rock. Name it.
a) Dal
b) Wular
c) Lonar
d) Chilka

HINDI FILMS

1. Amitabh Bachchan played the role of the father in the film
   Mahaan. Who played the role of his twin sons?
   a) Vinod Khanna
   b) Amitabh Bachchan
   c) Shatrughan Sinha
   d) Dharmendra

2. Which actor's birth name was Shivaji Rao Gaekwad?
   a) Chiranjeevi
   b) Mammootty
   c) Rajinikanth
   d) Kamal Haasan

3. Which was the first Indian film to get an Oscar nomination for
   Best Foreign Language Film?
   a) *Mother India*
   b) *Lagaan*

c) *Sholay*
d) *Salaam Bombay!*

4. Who worked as a chef in a restaurant and learnt martial arts in Bangkok before joining the film industry?
a) Shah Rukh Khan
b) Akshay Kumar
c) Dharmendra
d) Suniel Shetty

5. Whose favourite shooting spot in Switzerland, a lake in the Alpenrausch, was renamed in his honour?
a) Mahesh Bhatt
b) Yash Chopra
c) Raj Kapoor
d) Mani Ratnam

6. Who was the first actor to receive three consecutive Filmfare Awards in the Best Actor category?
a) Shah Rukh Khan
b) Dilip Kumar
c) Naseeruddin Shah
d) Amitabh Bachchan

7. Which actor was only six years old when he appeared in the film *Aasha*?
a) Aamir Khan
b) Salman Khan
c) Saif Ali Khan
d) Hrithik Roshan

8. On which author's short story is Satyajit Ray's film *Shatranj ke Khilari* based?
   a) Munshi Premchand
   b) Amrita Pritam
   c) Mahasweta Devi
   d) R.K. Narayan

9. Who directed the song sequences in *1942: A Love Story*?
   a) Vishal Bhardwaj
   b) Sanjay Leela Bhansali
   c) Karan Johar
   d) Farah Khan

10. Who was the first Indian actress to be on the jury of the Cannes Film Festival?
   a) Aishwarya Rai
   b) Sushmita Sen
   c) Priyanka Chopra
   d) Lara Dutta

11. Who is Saif Ali Khan's mother, also a famous actor?
   a) Nargis
   b) Sharmila Tagore
   c) Hema Malini
   d) Dimple Kapadia

12. My father won the Padma Bhushan in 1976. My wife won the Padma Shri in 1992. I have received the Padma Shri, the Padma Bhushan and the Padma Vibhushan. Who am I?
   a) Sunil Dutt
   b) Dilip Kumar

c) Rajesh Khanna
d) Amitabh Bachchan

13. Who made his directorial debut with *Kuch Kuch Hota Hai*?
    a) Farhan Akhtar
    b) Karan Johar
    c) Anurag Kashyap
    d) Ram Gopal Varma

14. Which famous king did Shah Rukh Khan play in a 2001 film directed by Santosh Sivan?
    a) Akbar
    b) Ashoka
    c) Shivaji
    d) Tipu Sultan

15. In the film *Sholay*, the role of Gabbar Singh was originally offered to ...
    a) Prem Chopra
    b) Danny Denzongpa
    c) Amrish Puri
    d) Pran

16. In a famous song from the film *Shree 420*, which accessory does Raj Kapoor describe as '*Roosi*'?
    a) *Patloon*
    b) *Topi*
    c) *Joota*
    d) *Kurta*

17. Which actress is common to the TV serial *Hum Paanch* and the film *Parineeta*?
a) Priyanka Chopra
b) Rani Mukherjee
c) Vidya Balan
d) Sushmita Sen

18. Which Indian film director was awarded the 1967 Ramon Magsaysay Award for Journalism, Literature and Creative Communication Arts?
a) Bimal Roy
b) Dev Anand
c) Shyam Benegal
d) Satyajit Ray

19. Who played the role of Saila in the 1987 film *Massey Sahib*?
a) Sonal Mansingh
b) Alka Yagnik
c) Arundhati Roy
d) P.T. Usha

20. The name of which of these films was taken from a poem by Harivansh Rai Bachchan?
a) *Muqaddar ka Sikandar*
b) *Ardh Satya*
c) *Agneepath*
d) *Aradhana*

HUMAN BODY

1. What does the formula 2123/2123 refer to?
   a) Fingers
   b) Blood pressure
   c) Pulse rate
   d) Teeth

2. What would you be having checked if a doctor used a Snellen chart?
   a) Eyes
   b) Ears
   c) Heart
   d) Lungs

3. What in the human body can be true, false and floating?
   a) Ribs
   b) Lungs

c) Kidneys
d) Teeth

4. Which is the largest organ in the human body, accounting for 16 per cent of the body weight?
   a) Heart
   b) Skin
   c) Brain
   d) Kidney

5. The first thing you would have to do is sit down and lean forward if you suddenly experienced what is medically called epistaxis. What would have happened?
   a) Hiccups
   b) Cramps
   c) Vertigo
   d) Nosebleed

6. What, in a doctor's prescription, is often expressed as 120/80?
   a) Duration for which the medicine has to be taken
   b) Strength of a medicine
   c) Blood pressure
   d) Eyesight

7. Simple, greenstick, Pott's and impacted are different types of ...
   a) Antibiotics
   b) Fractures
   c) Joints
   d) Veins

8. Which is the longest bone in the human body?
   a) Femur
   b) Ulna
   c) Sternum
   d) Radius

9. If healthy, which organ of the body will float in water and crackle when squeezed?
   a) Lung
   b) Brain
   c) Kidney
   d) Stomach

10. Which of these is caused by a sudden closure of the human glottis?
   a) Blink
   b) Yawn
   c) Sneeze
   d) Hiccup

11. The presence of which element makes the blood red?
   a) Copper
   b) Mercury
   c) Iron
   d) Potassium

12. With which organ in the human body is the word 'pulmonary' associated?
   a) Ears
   b) Eyes

c) Kidneys
d) Lungs

13. If your friends kept away from you because your axilla was smelling, which part of the body would be keeping them away?
a) Scalp
b) Armpits
c) Mouth
d) Feet

14. If your larynx was removed, what handicap would you suffer from?
a) Your left side would be paralysed.
b) You would not be able to hear.
c) You would be colourblind.
d) You would not be able to speak.

15. With which organ of the body is the pacemaker associated?
a) Ear
b) Kidney
c) Lung
d) Heart

16. Which is the most common blood type throughout the world?
a) B
b) A
c) AB
d) O

17. This J-shaped elastic sac is the widest part of the digestive system. It is the ...
a) Stomach
b) Pancreas
c) Liver
d) Small intestine

18. About 99 per cent of which element in the human body is held in the bones and teeth?
a) Potassium
b) Sodium
c) Calcium
d) Iron

19. Wilhelm Conrad Röntgen received the first Nobel Prize in Physics for his discovery of ...
a) Human blood groups
b) The human immunodeficiency virus
c) X-rays
d) Insulin

20. The hammer, anvil and stirrup are bones in which organ of the human body?
a) Ear
b) Nose
c) Eye
d) Lung

A TRIBUTE

Before the Bournvita Quiz Contest *shifted to television, it was hosted by the inimitable Ameen Sayani for many years. Here is a tribute to the golden voice of All India Radio.*

'It's the *Bournvita Quiz Contest!*'

The resounding voice echoed through a household as family members left what they were doing and rushed to sit in front of the wooden boxlike radio sets. Over the next half hour, every Sunday at noon, many such families would be enraptured as the host, Ameen Sayani, quizzed school students from the metropolitan cities. That was in the 1970s. And that captivating voice had already been radio's heartbeat for some years now.

Let's go back a couple of decades. Every Wednesday evening, in the 1950s, crores of people from Bombay (now Mumbai) to Jhumri Telaiya sat around their radio sets and tuned in to Radio Ceylon. They listened, engrossed, as a sonorous voice boomed,

'*Namaskar, behno aur bhaiyon, main aapka dost Ameen Sayani bol raha hoon.*' ('Hello, ladies and gentlemen, this is your friend Ameen Sayani speaking.') The programme was *Binaca Geetmala*.

His was the voice that not just entertained people but also unified the nation—breaking the barriers of region, language, religion and culture. At a time when most broadcasters used formal language and a serious style of delivery, Ameen Sayani used colloquial language and an informal presentation technique. His affable manner and gripping voice endeared him to the masses.

Ameen Sayani was born in 1932 into a family closely associated with the Independence Movement of India. He studied in New Era Public School in Bombay and The Scindia School in Gwalior. It was while he was in college (St Xavier's College, Mumbai) that his talent in the performing arts began to blossom.

From 1945 to 1960, he assisted his mother, Kulsum Sayani, with editing a fortnightly journal titled *Rahber*, which was initiated by Mahatma Gandhi. Working on this journal nurtured his knowledge of simple Hindustani language, which came in handy when he turned broadcaster.

Ameen Sayani's association with radio began when he was only seven years old. His elder brother, Hamid Sayani, was an eminent English broadcaster at the time. He introduced Ameen to the Bombay radio station of All India Radio (AIR) as a casual artiste in its English section. In 1949, Hamid also introduced Ameen to commercial broadcasting, for Radio Ceylon.

But Ameen's first big step in radio show production and presentation came with the Geetmala series, which was aired over the commercial Hindi Service of Radio Ceylon towards the end of 1952 and then shifted to All India Radio's Vividh Bharati network in 1989.

Initially, the duration of the show was half an hour. It was an experimental weekly jackpot show based on a random selection of songs. For Rs 25 a week, Ameen Sahab had to select the songs; produce, script and compère the programme; and process the mail. The first episode itself attracted about 9000 letters. But the competition was shelved in 1954, and was replaced by a one-hour countdown of the hit parade.

The new format, still on Radio Ceylon, was so popular that it drew millions of listeners from all over Asia, and even from East Africa. The programme not only promoted Hindi film music, but it also served to bring together the multilingual nation. When All India Radio suddenly decided to totally ban Hindi film music in the early fifties, it gave fillip to the popularity of the Geetmala programme. Ameen Sayani ran the show for nearly forty-five years.

After the untimely death of his brother, Hamid, in 1975, Ameen took over as the host of the *Bournvita Quiz Contest* and ran the show for eight years. The show was originally a live contest across multiple cities, before it became part of Vividh Bharati's weekly schedule on AIR in 1973. At that time, BQC featured teams of three school students each, who underwent a preliminary test in their respective schools to qualify for an all-India show in Bombay.

Ameen Sayani says he rehearsed meticulously to get all the proper nouns right. The questions were initially provided by the clients or agencies partnering with the show. According to him, the schools, usually from the four main Indian cities—Bombay, Delhi, Calcutta (now Kolkata) and Madras (now Chennai)—were well-versed in quizzing. Even so, he himself did thorough research before using a question.

Sayani recalls, 'Once a school team claimed they lost out in spite of them getting an answer right. The answer I had in hand was plaster of Paris and they had said gypsum. So they returned the next day with their schoolbooks and said, "Look! We had it right."[1] However, he cross-checked the answer with other encyclopedias several times before explaining to the students that gypsum is dehydrated to get plaster of Paris!

Years later, when the show shifted to TV, Ameen Sayani was one of the celebrity guests on the sets. He would ask four questions to the teams in his unmatched style.

———

Here's an interesting story. While All India Radio is credited for giving a platform to a lot of creative artists, not much of the population is aware that one of their most well-known presenters, Ameen Sayani, rejected our very own Big B!

In one of his interviews, Ameen revealed, 'It was somewhere in the late '60s when I used to do twenty shows a week, spending most of the day locked up in the sound studio as I was involved in every process of radio programming. One day, a young man named Amitabh Bachchan walked in without an appointment for a voice audition.'[2]

Referring to Big B as a 'thin man', Ameen didn't even realize that he was the same man whose persona had bowled him over when he'd watched *Anand* for the first time. 'I had not a second to spare for this thin man. He waited and left and came back a few more times. But I could not see him and kept telling him through my receptionist to take an appointment and come,' he added.

[1] Radhakrishnan M., 'The Bournvita Quiz Contest,' Livemint.com, 29 April 2015.
[2] Press Trust of India, 'When Ameen Sayani Shattered Big B's Dream of Becoming RJ,' *Indian Express*, 10 June 2014.

'Today, though I regret denying him an audition, I realize that what happened was for the best for the both of us. I would have been on the streets, and he would have got so much work on radio that Indian cinema would have lost its biggest star!' Sayani concluded.

What made Ameen Sayani so endearing to the masses, apart from his voice, was that he spoke conversationally, he interacted with his guests in a light-hearted and friendly manner and was never too shy to add a little humour.

The octogenarian radio presenter thinks that the 'cheap, accessible and wonderful' medium of radio is here to stay. 'The splurge of digital mediums will not result in the death of radio,' he confirms, dismissing music players and iPods. 'For me, radio was life and, in fact, that was the time when some of the senior broadcasters used to say that the greatest radio programmes are those that we can see. That is what I grew up in.'[3]

Over the years, Ameen Sayani has been associated with over 54,000 programmes and 19,000 jingles. Even today, he is one of the most imitated announcers. He lives in Mumbai and leads a quiet life.

---

[3] Indo-Asian News Service, 'Radio As a Medium Will Never Die: Octogenarian Ameen Sayani,' *Indian Express*, 1 July 2014.

1. If the Republic Day parade starts from Raisina Hill near the Rashtrapati Bhavan, where does it end?
   a) Parliament House
   b) Red Fort
   c) Purana Qila
   d) India Gate

2. What does Bholu, the mascot of Indian Railways, hold in his hand?
   a) A lantern
   b) A stick
   c) A bell
   d) A flag

3. In 1933, who gave the name Amartya to Amartya Sen, the famous economist?
   a) Mahatma Gandhi

b) S.D. Burman
c) Rabindranath Tagore
d) Satyajit Ray

4. Which entity of national importance was designed by Pingali Venkayya?
    a) The Indian national flag
    b) The rupee symbol
    c) The Rashtrapati Bhavan
    d) The All India Radio logo

5. Traditionally, who uses a gold broom and acts as 'sweeper to the gods' at the Puri Rath Yatra?
    a) The head priest
    b) The raja of Puri
    c) The oldest pilgrim
    d) The chief minister of Odisha

6. In the language panel of contemporary Indian banknotes, what is the last language in which the denomination is written?
    a) Nepali
    b) Urdu
    c) Tamil
    d) Telugu

7. Which famous song, composed by Muhammad Iqbal, is also known as 'Tarana-e-Hindi'?
    a) 'Saare Jahaan Se Achcha'
    b) 'Kadam Kadam Badhaye Jaa'
    c) 'Mera Rang De Basanti Chola'
    d) 'Maa Tujhe Salaam'

8. *Something Beautiful for God* is a book by Malcolm Muggeridge. Who is the subject of the book?
   a) Mother Teresa
   b) Sundarlal Bahuguna
   c) Baba Amte
   d) Vinoba Bhave

9. What is the state tree of Kerala?
   a) Banyan
   b) Coconut palm
   c) Neem
   d) Sandal

10. The Golden Chariot train is named after the famous Stone Chariot in Hampi. In which state is Hampi located?
    a) Kerala
    b) Tamil Nadu
    c) Karnataka
    d) Maharashtra

11. At which monument did Jawaharlal Nehru hoist the national flag of India on 15 August 1947?
    a) Parliament House
    b) The Rashtrapati Bhavan
    c) India Gate
    d) Red Fort

12. The inhabitants of a village named Mattur in Karnataka . . .
    a) Speak Sanskrit on a regular basis
    b) Never lock their doors

c) Live on top of banyan trees

d) Never leave the village

13. In which Indian state is the Surajkund Crafts Fair held?

a) Punjab

b) Andhra Pradesh

c) Haryana

d) Bihar

14. In India, what took place between 19 November and 4 December 1982?

a) The first census

b) The first general elections

c) The ninth Asian Games

d) The Kumbh Mela

15. Which festival connects Bohag (or Rongali), Kati (or Kongali) and Magh (or Bhogali)?

a) Lohri

b) Bihu

c) Baisakhi

d) Pongal

16. The name of which festival means 'boiling over' in Tamil?

a) Ugadi

b) Diwali

c) Pongal

d) Holi

17. Which animal is worshipped at the famous Karni Mata Temple in Rajasthan?
   a) Rats
   b) Monkeys
   c) Cats
   d) Chameleons

18. According to the 2011 census, which state has the highest literacy rate in India?
   a) Kerala
   b) Uttar Pradesh
   c) Tamil Nadu
   d) Mizoram

19. Shanti Van is the samadhi of which prime minister of India?
   a) Jawaharlal Nehru
   b) Indira Gandhi
   c) Lal Bahadur Shastri
   d) Charan Singh

20. What was first sung at the Calcutta session of the Indian National Congress on 27 December 1911?
   a) 'Vande Mataram'
   b) 'Saare Jahaan Se Achcha'
   c) 'Jana Gana Mana'
   d) 'Kadam Kadam Badhaye Jaa'

INDIAN CUISINE

1. Which food item is made with a hard-boiled egg that resembles a pair of eyes when cut lengthwise?
   a) Paneer pasanda
   b) Nargisi kofta
   c) Gatte ki sabzi
   d) Shahi tukda

2. What did the first Nizam choose as the official emblem of the Asaf Jahi dynasty?
   a) Shami kebab
   b) Laddoo
   c) Samosa
   d) Kulcha

3. In 1877, what was first produced in Bikaner during the reign of Maharaja Dungar Singh?
   a) Rasgulla

b) Bhujia
c) Thekua
d) Haleem

4. With which Indian community would you associate the preparation called dhansak?
   a) Sikh
   b) Jewish
   c) Parsi
   d) Christian

5. Sorpotel is a speciality of which state of India?
   a) Odisha
   b) Kerala
   c) Goa
   d) Sikkim

6. Mysore pak is a kind of . . .
   a) Bread
   b) Sweet
   c) Soup
   d) Fritter

7. In India, with which food item was Operation Flood associated?
   a) Mustard oil
   b) Milk
   c) Sugar cane juice
   d) Rose water

8. If you were adding Indian dates to your curry, what would you be adding?
   a) Tamarind
   b) Turmeric
   c) Garlic
   d) Ginger

9. Dum pukht cuisine was introduced during the reign of which king over 200 years ago in Awadh?
   a) Wajid Ali Shah
   b) Asaf-ud-Daulah
   c) Osman Ali Khan
   d) Aurangzeb

10. Which of these vegetables forms the main ingredient of batata vada?
   a) Cauliflower
   b) Cabbage
   c) Potato
   d) Eggplant

11. Which kebab is named after a small town in Uttar Pradesh, famous for a train robbery in 1925?
   a) Galouti kebab
   b) Shami kebab
   c) Kakori kebab
   d) Chelo kebab

12. The name of which sweet comes from a Persian word meaning 'icy' or 'snowy'?
   a) Laddoo

b) Barfi
c) Rasgulla
d) Jalebi

13. In which state did rogan josh originate?
   a) Uttar Pradesh
   b) Himachal Pradesh
   c) Jammu and Kashmir
   d) Andhra Pradesh

14. What is the main ingredient of shahi tukda?
   a) Bread
   b) Cottage cheese
   c) Vermicelli
   d) Rice

15. With which Indian state is Chettinad cuisine associated?
   a) Kerala
   b) Tamil Nadu
   c) Uttar Pradesh
   d) Andhra Pradesh

16. What is a *bukhari*?
   a) An oven
   b) A style of cutting onions
   c) A paneer dish
   d) Another name for orange

17. Which of these is not an Indian sweetmeat?
   a) Rasbhara
   b) Rasmalai

c) Raskadam
d) Rasam

18. What are Totapuri, Dussehri, Neelam and Himsagar types of?
a) Banana
b) Mango
c) Orange
d) Apple

19. Which famous cookery show host is the author of *Khazana of Indian Vegetarian Recipes*?
a) Sanjeev Kapoor
b) Tarla Dalal
c) Niru Gupta
d) Madhur Jaffrey

20. What kind of creature is the Bombay duck?
a) Duck
b) Fish
c) Crab
d) Partridge

INDIAN HISTORY

1. Even though Mahatma Gandhi tried for many years, what was finally found by Gangabehn Majmundar?
   a) The word Harijan
   b) Wooden sandals
   c) Charkha
   d) Rimmed spectacles

2. Who gave the Koh-i-noor diamond its name?
   a) Nadir Shah
   b) Shah Jahan
   c) Ranjit Singh
   d) Ghiyasuddin Balban

3. According to legend, the great demand for whose ashes led to the creation of a water tank in Pawapuri?
   a) Lord Mahavira
   b) Mahatma Gandhi

    c) Gautama Buddha

    d) Raj Kapoor

4. Which present-day Indian city did Job Charnock 'find' in 1690?

    a) Mumbai

    b) Chennai

    c) Kolkata

    d) Cuttack

5. After which Indian was a stretch of Michigan Avenue in Chicago renamed?

    a) Ishwar Chandra Vidyasagar

    b) Ram Mohan Roy

    c) Sri Aurobindo

    d) Swami Vivekananda

6. Who spent his last 144 days at Old Birla House on No. 5, Tees January Marg, New Delhi?

    a) Mahatma Gandhi

    b) Jawaharlal Nehru

    c) Rajendra Prasad

    d) Vallabhbhai Patel

7. What animal adorned most of Tipu Sultan's possessions?

    a) King cobra

    b) Butterfly

    c) Tiger

    d) Horse

8. The five Ks of Sikhism are kangha, kesh, kachcha, kirpan and . . .

    a) Kara

b) Kapda
c) Kitaab
d) Kadhai

9. If you were reading the teachings of Viswambhara Mishra, whose work would you be reading?
   a) Ram Mohan Roy
   b) Swami Vivekananda
   c) Chaitanya Mahaprabhu
   d) Sri Aurobindo

10. How was Ram Mohan Roy rewarded by the king of Delhi for going to England and pleading the king's case?
    a) He was made the chief courtier of the emperor's court.
    b) He was made principal of Sanskrit College.
    c) He was married off to the emperor's daughter.
    d) He was conferred with the title of Raja.

11. The oldest capital of which south Indian dynasty was Uraiyur (now Tiruchirapalli)?
    a) Chola
    b) Pandya
    c) Chera
    d) Chalukya

12. Who was appointed governor general of all French establishments in India in the 1740s?
    a) Joseph Francois Dupleix
    b) Gabriel Hanotaux
    c) Jean-Baptiste Eugène Abel
    d) Louis Jean Girod

13. Which is the oldest Veda?
   a) Yajur Veda
   b) Atharva Veda
   c) Sama Veda
   d) Rig Veda

14. Name the Chinese pilgrim who came to India during the reign of Chandragupta II.
   a) Megasthenes
   b) Fa-Hien
   c) Tavernier
   d) Hiuen Tsang

15. In which city was the first Buddhist council held?
   a) Vaishali
   b) Rajagriha
   c) Pataliputra
   d) Kannauj

16. Which portfolio did Indira Gandhi hold in the government of Lal Bahadur Shastri?
   a) Ministry of Home Affairs
   b) Ministry of External Affairs
   c) Ministry of Information and Broadcasting
   d) Ministry of Atomic Energy

17. In 1516, who was married to Bhoj Raj, the crown prince of Mewar?
   a) Mira Bai
   b) Rani Lakshmibai

c) Rani Padmini
d) Jodha Bai

18. Which was the first dynasty of the Delhi Sultanate period?
    a) Lodhi
    b) Khilji
    c) Slave
    d) Sayyid

19. After her first son was born in 304 BCE, Queen Subhadrangi said that her life was 'without sorrow'. What was her son's name?
    a) Humayun
    b) Chandragupta
    c) Ashoka
    d) Shivaji

20. Who gave Margaret Elizabeth Noble the name Nivedita, meaning 'the dedicated one'?
    a) Mahatma Gandhi
    b) Rabindranath Tagore
    c) Swami Vivekananda
    d) Mother Teresa

INDIAN LEADERS

1. Who has been the longest-serving prime minister of India?
   a) Jawaharlal Nehru
   b) Lal Bahadur Shastri
   c) Indira Gandhi
   d) Morarji Desai

2. Who became the chairman of the drafting committee of the Constitution of India on 29 August 1947?
   a) Vallabhbhai Patel
   b) Rajendra Prasad
   c) B.R. Ambedkar
   d) Bal Gangadhar Tilak

3. Which of these events disturbed Sarojini Naidu so much that she gave up writing poems?
   a) The Jallianwala Bagh massacre
   b) The Chauri Chaura incident

    c)   The execution of Khudiram Bose

    d)   The death of Mahatma Gandhi

4. Who was the only Indian governor general of independent India?
    a)   Vallabhbhai Patel
    b)   Gopal Krishna Gokhale
    c)   Syed Ahmed Khan
    d)   C. Rajagopalachari

5. Vijay Ghat is the memorial ground of which famous leader?
    a)   Lal Bahadur Shastri
    b)   Rajiv Gandhi
    c)   Jagjivan Ram
    d)   Ram Manohar Lohia

6. President Zakir Husain was the first Indian President to . . .
    a)   Make an amendment
    b)   Resign from office
    c)   Visit the Siachen Glacier
    d)   Die in office

7. Who inaugurated the Government of Free India in Singapore in the early 1940s?
    a)   Mahatma Gandhi
    b)   Dadabhai Naoroji
    c)   Subhas Chandra Bose
    d)   Jawaharlal Nehru

8. In India, whose birth anniversary is celebrated as Sadbhavna Diwas and death anniversary as Anti-Terrorism Day?
    a)   Rajiv Gandhi

b)   Indira Gandhi
c)   Giani Zail Singh
d)   Rajendra Prasad

9. What did Atal Bihari Vajpayee add to the slogan *Jai Jawan,*
    Jai Kisan' after the Pokhran tests?
    a)   *Jai Anusandhan*
    b)   *Jai Vigyan*
    c)   *Jai Bhagwan*
    d)   *Jai Hindustan*

10. Who is also known as the Grand Old Man of India?
    a)   Dadabhai Naoroji
    b)   Lala Lajpat Rai
    c)   Bal Gangadhar Tilak
    d)   Gopal Krishna Gokhale

11. Fill in the blank to complete this equation by Acharya Vinoba
    Bhave: 'Spirituality plus _____ = Sarvodaya'.
    a)   Literature
    b)   Science
    c)   Politics
    d)   History

12. Which prime minister never faced the Parliament, even
    though he was in office for 171 days?
    a)   Charan Singh
    b)   Gulzari Lal Nanda
    c)   Chandra Shekhar
    d)   H.D. Deve Gowda

13. Who was Jawaharlal Nehru's famous sister?
   a) Sarojini Naidu
   b) Vijaya Lakshmi Pandit
   c) Rajkumari Amrit Kaur
   d) Annie Besant

14. Which President of India wrote *India 2020* and *Ignited Minds*?
   a) Pratibha Patil
   b) Pranab Mukherjee
   c) A.P.J. Abdul Kalam
   d) K.R. Narayanan

15. Who is the only prime minister of India to have signed a banknote?
   a) Manmohan Singh
   b) V.P. Singh
   c) Inder Kumar Gujral
   d) P.V. Narasimha Rao

16. Whose autobiography was translated from Gujarati into English by Mahadev Desai?
   a) Sucheta Kripalani
   b) Sarojini Naidu
   c) Vijaya Lakshmi Pandit
   d) Mahatma Gandhi

17. Who was the first deputy prime minister of India?
   a) Abul Kalam Azad
   b) Lala Lajpat Rai
   c) Vallabhbhai Patel
   d) Charan Singh

18. On whose birth anniversary is National Education Day celebrated in India?
   a) Vallabhbhai Patel
   b) B.R. Ambedkar
   c) Abul Kalam Azad
   d) Bal Gangadhar Tilak

19. Who was professor of Eastern religions and ethics at the University of Oxford in England from 1936 to 1952?
   a) S. Radhakrishnan
   b) Lala Lajpat Rai
   c) Dadabhai Naoroji
   d) Vallabhbhai Patel

20. Who founded and edited the Hindi weekly *Desh*?
   a) Rajendra Prasad
   b) Jawaharlal Nehru
   c) Lala Lajpat Rai
   d) Abul Kalam Azad

INDIAN LITERATURE

1. Which author's collection of short stories, titled *Soz-e-Watan*, was banned by the British?
    a) Mulk Raj Anand
    b) Premchand
    c) Amrita Pritam
    d) Mahadevi Verma

2. In *The Jungle Book*, who was the 'great grey lone wolf'?
    a) Akela
    b) Baloo
    c) Kaa
    d) Bagheera

3. Rabindranath Tagore wrote the national anthem of which of these countries?
    a) Nepal
    b) Bangladesh

c) Sri Lanka
d) Pakistan

4. *Hitopadesha* is a collection of stories based on which ancient work?
   a) The Natyashastra
   b) The Arthashastra
   c) *Panchatantra*
   d) Rig Veda

5. Who was the first person to win the Jnanpith Award?
   a) Raja Rao
   b) R.K. Narayan
   c) Amrita Pritam
   d) G. Sankara Kurup

6. *The Rigveda Samhita* contains about 10,552 mantras, classified into ten books called ...
   a) Chakras
   b) Sutras
   c) Parvas
   d) Mandalas

7. The Jataka Tales are stories about the former lives of ...
   a) Krishna
   b) Gautama Buddha
   c) Lord Mahavira
   d) Guru Nanak

8. Kamban, Krittibas and Tulsidas have all written different versions of which work?
   a) Manimekalai
   b) The Mahabharata
   c) The Ramayana
   d) Ashtadhyayi

9. For which work did R.K. Narayan receive the Sahitya Akademi Award in 1960?
   a) *Malgudi Days*
   b) *The Guide*
   c) *Swami and Friends*
   d) *The Painter of Signs*

10. Which work by Kalidasa recounts the legend of Rama's ancestors and descendants?
    a) *Malavikagnimitram*
    b) *Kumarasambhava*
    c) *Raghuvansham*
    d) *Ritusamhara*

11. Which book is sometimes referred to as the fifth Veda?
    a) The Arthashastra
    b) The Natyashastra
    c) The Sushruta Samhita
    d) Ashtadhyayi

12. Which Indian poet is commonly referred to as the Father of Modern Hindi?
    a) Suryakant Tripathi 'Nirala'
    b) Bharatendu Harishchandra

c) Makhanlal Chaturvedi
d) Maithili Sharan Gupt

13. Which author's birth name was Dhanpat Rai?
a) Munshi Premchand
b) Mulk Raj Anand
c) Khushwant Singh
d) Bhisham Sahni

14. 'Palanquin Bearers' is a poem by . . .
a) Rabindranath Tagore
b) Sarojini Naidu
c) Ruskin Bond
d) Mahadevi Verma

15. On which author's story is the 2003 film *Pinjar* based?
a) Vikram Seth
b) Sarat Chandra Chattopadhyay
c) Mulk Raj Anand
d) Amrita Pritam

16. Which story revolves around the fortunes of four families: the Mehras, the Kapoors, the Khans and the Chatterjis?
a) *The Hungry Tide*
b) *The Namesake*
c) *Train to Pakistan*
d) *A Suitable Boy*

17. In *Kumarasambhava*, Kalidasa describes the story of . . .
a) Shiva and Parvati
b) Arjuna and Draupadi

c) Krishna and Rukmini
d) Akbar and Jodha

18. Which author's first novel is titled *The Room on the Roof*?
a) Ruskin Bond
b) R.K. Narayan
c) Rudyard Kipling
d) Raja Rao

19. Fill in the missing word in the extract taken from a poem by Nissim Ezekiel: 'Thank God the _____ picked on me/And spared my children'.
a) Lion
b) Snake
c) Scorpion
d) Tiger

20. Which was the first Sanskrit work chosen for English translation by the Asiatic Society?
a) Rig Veda
b) The Mahabharata
c) The Ramayana
d) The Natyashastra

INTERNATIONAL FILMS

1. Who was the first actor to appear on the cover of *Time* magazine?
   a) James Dean
   b) Charlie Chaplin
   c) John Wayne
   d) Gregory Peck

2. Which series of films features characters such as Princess Leia, Yoda, R2-D2 and Luke Skywalker?
   a) Harry Potter
   b) Indiana Jones
   c) Star Wars
   d) Star Trek

3. What do you call a western film made cheaply in Europe by an Italian director?
   a) Pizza Western

b) Salsa Western
c) Macaroni Western
d) Spaghetti Western

4. In 1983, who received the Oscar for Best Costume Design along with John Mollo?
a) Satyajit Ray
b) Bhanu Athaiya
c) Ritu Kumar
d) Ruth Prawer Jhabvala

5. Which Indian was the music director of the film *Shakespeare Wallah*?
a) S.D. Burman
b) Ravi Shankar
c) Bismillah Khan
d) Satyajit Ray

6. Kathryn Bigelow became the first woman to win an Oscar in the Best Director category for...
a) *The Hurt Locker*
b) *American Sniper*
c) *Black Hawk Down*
d) *Saving Private Ryan*

7. The film *Enter the Dragon* revolves around...
a) Track and field sports
b) Board games
c) Martial arts
d) Racquet sports

8. Name the American President and his wife who acted in the 1957 film *Hellcats of the Navy*.
   a) John and Jacqueline Kennedy
   b) Eleanor and Franklin D. Roosevelt
   c) Jimmy and Rosalynn Carter
   d) Ronald and Nancy Reagan

9. In 1999, the US Department of Defense gave its highest civilian award to this director. Who was the director?
   a) Steven Spielberg
   b) George Lucas
   c) Rob Reiner
   d) Mel Gibson

10. Which character did Basil Rathbone play in the film *The Hound of the Baskervilles*?
   a) Sherlock Holmes
   b) James Bond
   c) Indiana Jones
   d) Hercule Poirot

11. The 1962 film *To Kill a Mockingbird* was based on a novel by ...
   a) Charlotte Bronte
   b) Pearl S. Buck
   c) Margaret Mitchell
   d) Harper Lee

12. Which film launched the Marvel Cinematic Universe?
   a) *Captain America: The First Avenger*
   b) *Iron Man*

c) *Guardians of the Galaxy: Vol. 1*
d) *The Avengers*

13. Which 1982 film made it into the Guinness World Records for the largest number of extras in one scene?
   a) *E.T. the Extra-Terrestrial*
   b) *Blade Runner*
   c) *Gandhi*
   d) *Poltergeist*

14. Which character is common to Sean Connery, Roger Moore, George Lazenby and Pierce Brosnan?
   a) Sherlock Holmes
   b) James Bond
   c) Hercule Poirot
   d) Indiana Jones

15. Which actor was initially rejected by agents for having a weird body, a funny accent and a very long name?
   a) George Clooney
   b) Sylvester Stallone
   c) Arnold Schwarzenegger
   d) Gérard Depardieu

16. What does the Oscar statuette of the knight stand on?
   a) A reel of film
   b) A torch
   c) A drum
   d) A wooden box

17. Who played the role of Itzhak Stern in the 1993 film *Schindler's List*?
- a) Liam Neeson
- b) Ralph Fiennes
- c) Ben Kingsley
- d) Jonathan Sagall

18. With which series of films would you associate the phrase 'May the force be with you'?
- a) Star Trek
- b) Star Wars
- c) Alien
- d) Planet of the Apes

19. Which Hollywood 1956 classic has the line 'So let it be written, so let it be done'?
- a) *Spartacus*
- b) *Lawrence of Arabia*
- c) *Ben-Hur*
- d) *The Ten Commandments*

20. Which famous Steven Spielberg film begins with a woman being killed by a great white shark?
- a) *Saving Private Ryan*
- b) *Raiders of the Lost Ark*
- c) *Jaws*
- d) *Jurassic Park*

KINGS AND QUEENS

1. When Shivaji was imprisoned by Aurangzeb in Agra, how did he escape?
   a) He hid in a basket of sweets.
   b) He pretended to be mad and was taken to an asylum.
   c) He pretended to be dead and was buried.
   d) He killed a guard and donned his clothes.

2. Which king called himself Devanampiya Piyadasi, or Beloved of the Gods?
   a) Harshavardhana
   b) Prithviraj Chauhan
   c) Maharana Pratap
   d) Ashoka

3. How is Princess Manikarnika better known in history?
   a) Rani Padmini
   b) Jodha Bai

c) Rani Lakshmibai
d) Nur Jahan

4. In India, which dynasty issued gold coins for the first time in substantial numbers?
a) Chola
b) Kushana
c) Chera
d) Pratihara

5. In 643 CE, who summoned the Kannauj assembly in honour of Hiuen Tsang?
a) Prithviraj Chauhan
b) Ashoka
c) Kanishka
d) Harshavardhana

6. Which dynasty came to an end with the invasion of Malik Kafur in the early fourteenth century?
a) Chera
b) Chola
c) Pandya
d) Pratihara

7. Which famous sultan of Delhi did Shihabuddin Umar succeed briefly in 1316?
a) Alauddin Khilji
b) Muhammad bin Tughlaq
c) Razia Sultana
d) Ibrahim Lodhi

8. In 1813–14, what was returned to India through the efforts of Ranjit Singh, the king of Lahore?
   a) The Peacock Throne
   b) The Koh-i-noor diamond
   c) His title
   d) Akbar's sword

9. In Greek sources, who is referred to as Amitrochates, Greek for the Sanskrit *amitraghata*, meaning 'destroyer of foes'?
   a) Kirtivarman II
   b) Chandragupta Maurya
   c) Kanishka
   d) Bindusara

10. Which was the first empire to unite a great part of India under a central authority?
   a) Maurya
   b) Gupta
   c) Pratihara
   d) Pandya

11. Robert Clive fought Siraj-ud-Daulah in the Battle of Plassey in 1757. In which present-day Indian state is Plassey located?
   a) Uttar Pradesh
   b) Bihar
   c) Odisha
   d) West Bengal

12. On being informed that there was no warfare in paradise, who said, 'How then can there be any delights there?'
   a) Nadir Shah

b) Mahmud of Ghazni
c) Muhammad Ghori
d) Ghiyasuddin Balban

13. Who introduced the practice of *sijda* (prostration) and *paibos* (kissing the monarch's feet) in court as normal forms of salutation to the king?
    a) Mubarak Shah
    b) Jalal-ud-din Firoz Khilji
    c) Muhammad bin Tughlaq
    d) Ghiyasuddin Balban

14. Chanakya was adviser to which famous ruler?
    a) Harshavardhana
    b) Chandragupta Maurya
    c) Kanishka
    d) Krishnadevaraya

15. Who invaded Chittorgarh in 1303 because of his passionate desire to abduct Rani Padmini?
    a) Alauddin Khilji
    b) Qutb-ud-din Aibak
    c) Firuz Shah Tughlaq
    d) Khizr Khan

16. What was the name of Maharana Pratap's famous horse?
    a) Chetak
    b) Bucephalus
    c) Kantak
    d) Pawan

17. Who was the first woman to sit on the throne of Delhi?
   a) Chand Bibi
   b) Nur Jahan
   c) Razia Sultan
   d) Rani Lakshmibai

18. Which city was ruled by the Cholas from 920 CE till the beginning of the thirteenth century?
   a) Guntur
   b) Mysore
   c) Madurai
   d) Kannauj

19. The Bhavani Talwar belonged to which famous Indian ruler?
   a) Shivaji
   b) Rana Sanga
   c) Maharana Pratap
   d) Ashoka

20. The historian Bana wrote about which Indian king?
   a) Mahapadma Nanda
   b) Samudragupta
   c) Chandragupta Maurya
   d) Harshavardhana

LANGUAGE

1. Which word links a widely spoken language, a type of duck and a kind of orange?
   a) Polish
   b) Dutch
   c) Mandarin
   d) Persian

2. In which figure of speech is a thing compared with another thing of a different kind?
   a) Alliteration
   b) Simile
   c) Oxymoron
   d) Hyperbole

3. In America, this punctuation mark is called a period. What is it called in India?
   a) Apostrophe

b) Comma
c) Full stop
d) Colon

4. According to the phrase, whom do you pay when you rob Peter?
   a) Pablo
   b) Patrick
   c) Philip
   d) Paul

5. Which word is used to denote a lover of books or a book collector?
   a) Francophile
   b) Cinephile
   c) Bibliophile
   d) Astrophile

6. If you were talking about horses, which of these words are you most likely to use?
   a) Porcine
   b) Equine
   c) Feline
   d) Asinine

7. Who is a cruciverbalist?
   a) An expert at solving crossword puzzles
   b) A person who talks too much
   c) A tightrope walker
   d) A quizmaster's assistant

8. According to the proverb, what does a rolling stone not gather?
a) Moss
b) Dust
c) Floss
d) Soil

9. A gentleman's agreement is an agreement ...
a) That is signed by single men
b) That is signed by Wimbledon players
c) Based upon trust rather than law
d) Drafted by non-lawyers

10. What word would link a person who is mean with money, Donald Duck's uncle and a character in *A Christmas Carol*?
a) Scrooge
b) Micawber
c) Fezziwig
d) Fagin

11. Which punctuation mark is derived from a Greek word meaning 'limb' or 'clause'?
a) Comma
b) Apostrophe
c) Colon
d) Question mark

12. What do you call the phrase written in memory of a person who has died, especially as an inscription on a tombstone?
a) Trigraph
b) Epigraph

c) Cenotaph
d) Epitaph

13. What do you call a squirrel's nest?
   a) Lair
   b) Drey
   c) Den
   d) Coop

14. 'Couch potato' is a . . .
   a) Term used for a person who watches a lot of TV with no exercise
   b) Type of sweet potato
   c) Type of round cushion for couches
   d) Term used for farmers

15. What would you find in a mermaid's purse?
   a) Small plants
   b) Eggs of a small shark
   c) A shrimp's heart
   d) A pearl

16. What is the last letter of the Greek alphabet?
   a) Omega
   b) Epsilon
   c) Gamma
   d) Sigma

17. Euphemistically, what is a marble orchard?
   a) A shop that sells coloured playing marbles
   b) A graveyard, because of the marble tombstones

c) A toilet decorated with glazed tiles
d) A garden where leeches are grown

18. Which word, meaning 'a short official note', 'memorandum' or 'voucher', typically recording a sum owed, comes from a Hindi word meaning 'note' or 'pass'?
    a) Chit
    b) Bill
    c) Receipt
    d) Ticket

19. The phrase 'red tape' signifies official formality and delay. The term originated from the system of . . .
    a) Securing official documents with red or pink tape
    b) Using books of accounts with red covers
    c) Using red flags to signify danger
    d) Marking the documents with red ink

20. Which sign would you use in place of the word 'and'?
    a) Ampersand
    b) Hash
    c) Exclamation mark
    d) Asterisk

LEADERS OF THE WORLD

1. Who was Europe's first woman prime minister?
   a) Mary McAleese
   b) Violeta Chamorro
   c) Margaret Thatcher
   d) Angela Merkel

2. With which leader is the famous Gettysburg Address associated?
   a) George Washington
   b) Abraham Lincoln
   c) Winston Churchill
   d) Martin Luther King

3. In 1973, who was re-elected President of Argentina after eighteen years in exile?
   a) Alejandro Agustín Lanusse
   b) Juan Perón

c) Héctor José Cámpora
d) Raúl Alberto Lastiri

4. Which surname is shared by the man who discovered Tutankhamen's tomb and the thirty-ninth US President?
    a) Carter
    b) Clinton
    c) Jefferson
    d) Jackson

5. Until 1961, whose body was preserved in Lenin's mausoleum at the Red Square in Moscow?
    a) Adolf Hitler
    b) Fidel Castro
    c) Ivan the Terrible
    d) Joseph Stalin

6. Mustafa Kemal Atatürk was the founder and first President of the Republic of . . .
    a) Jordan
    b) Syria
    c) Turkey
    d) Armenia

7. Golda Meir was a founder and fourth prime minister of . . .
    a) New Zealand
    b) Israel
    c) Myanmar
    d) South Sudan

8. Who was awarded the Nobel Peace Prize in 1991 but gave the acceptance speech in 2012?
   a) Aung San Suu Kyi
   b) Ellen Johnson Sirleaf
   c) Nelson Mandela
   d) Amartya Sen

9. The capital of which African country is named after US President James Monroe?
   a) Guinea
   b) Lesotho
   c) Sierra Leone
   d) Liberia

10. Who was the chairman of the People's Republic of China from 1949 to 1959?
    a) Ho Chi Minh
    b) Sun Yat-sen
    c) Mao Zedong
    d) Chiang Kai-shek

11. Who was the British prime minister when India became independent?
    a) Clement Attlee
    b) Winston Churchill
    c) Harold Macmillan
    d) Anthony Eden

12. In 2005, who became the first female chancellor of Germany?
    a) Ursula von der Leyen
    b) Angela Merkel

c) Christine Lagarde
d) Sarah Palin

13. Who sang 'The Song for Peace' minutes before he was assassinated?
a) John F. Kennedy
b) Abraham Lincoln
c) Yitzhak Rabin
d) Mahatma Gandhi

14. Whose autobiography is titled *Long Walk To Freedom*?
a) Jacob Zuma
b) Thabo Mbeki
c) Kofi Annan
d) Nelson Mandela

15. How is Vladimir Ilyich Ulyanov popularly known?
a) Putin
b) Lenin
c) Stalin
d) Ataturk

16. Who coined the term 'United Nations'?
a) Winston Churchill
b) Franklin Roosevelt
c) Theodore Roosevelt
d) Adolf Hitler

17. Who is the famous daughter of Sheikh Mujibur Rahman?
a) Khaleda Zia
b) Sheikh Hasina Wazed

c) Benazir Bhutto
d) Megawati Sukarnoputri

18. Which leader, born in Braunau am Inn, failed to secure entry into the Academy of Fine Arts, Vienna, twice?
a) Adolf Hitler
b) Benito Mussolini
c) Winston Churchill
d) Joseph Stalin

19. In which category did Winston Churchill receive the Nobel Prize?
a) Medicine
b) Peace
c) Literature
d) Chemistry

20. Which famous leader had a horse named Marengo?
a) Julius Caesar
b) Napoleon
c) Alexander
d) Horatio Nelson

FROM BQC TO THE OSCARS

AN ESSAY BY TESS JOSEPH

Tess Joseph has made us all proud. She started off as a production executive on BQC in the early 2000s, and today she is a well-known casting director, both in Bollywood and Hollywood. Having started with Mira Nair's The Namesake, she recently selected the Indian cast for the Oscar-nominated film Lion. In this essay from 2017, Tess takes us through her memorable journey, from BQC to the Oscars.

The year was 2000, and I was the new kid on the *Bournvita Quiz Contest*. The office was an apartment, and the team—just fourteen people! I had grown up with this show, and I remember the awesome feeling I'd get when I'd tell people that I work on the *Bournvita Quiz Contest*. Even now, seventeen years later, it fills me with pride! Because BQC is part of my DNA. In fact, the second question I still ask anyone new is 'Tell me, which school did you go to?'—you see, I've inherited a secret deciphering superpower after seven years of working with thousands of children from across sixty-six cities and seven countries.

Without BQC, and the motley crew of Derek O'Brien & Associates, movies would have never found me. I started as a production executive on BQC, and, trust me, I've played every role in the book—from ensuring that the students eat breakfast and coordinating celebrity appearances to co-directing the show. And between Rila and Derek, I had a freedom that many could only dream of when they're fresh off the college boat.

I took the show from an indoor 'nerdy' quiz to more than a contest. It became an experience and aspiration for every student achiever out there. Today, names like Deepika Pallikal and Palak Muchhal are an inspiration to millions of young girls. Truth is, if they look back ever so gently, they will find that BQC was the first platform that showcased their talent. From Sri Lanka to Spiti, from the brightest minds to the best athletes and musicians, BQC grew over the years, and I did too.

In 2005, I took my first sabbatical; I was casting for Mira Nair's *The Namesake*. I was casting without a clue of the names or faces of any contemporary Bengali actor in Kolkata. After reading the script, I would avidly watch the local channels and movies on a VHS player, ready to record any face I found interesting. The next day, I would inundate my research team with questions like 'Who is this?' and 'Who is that?' and they, of course, knew all the answers! Then I'd take my list to our studio, Sunrise—a place I called my second home, because I've seen many a sunrise and sunset editing BQC in that office—and Mr Bhura would help me collate contact details. *The Namesake* propelled my casting career, and it was possible thanks to the ironclad support system of my BQC team. Now when I look back, maybe that was when I began to notice and hone young talent. Maybe I was a casting director all along, and BQC is where its seeds were first sown.

Sometimes it's the journey that teaches you a lot about your destination. Here I am today, still reeling from a magical year of being the only Indian casting director to be invited by the Academy Awards for outstanding contribution to a Best Picture nominee—*Lion*.

MIXED BAG

1. Which film by Satyajit Ray was completed when Dr B.C. Roy, former chief minister of West Bengal, provided funds from the Public Works Department, on the grounds that *path* ('road') was a matter within the PWD's jurisdiction?
   a) *Pather Panchali*
   b) *Jalsaghar*
   c) *Sonar Kella*
   d) *Mahapurush*

2. Arabica and robusta are two main varieties of . . .
   a) Tea
   b) Coffee
   c) Silk
   d) Biryani

3. According to Thomas Alva Edison, what is 1 per cent inspiration and 99 per cent perspiration?
 a) Victory
 b) Genius
 c) Greatness
 d) Success

4. In 1973, which country produced stamps in the shape of records that could be played?
 a) Japan
 b) Pakistan
 c) Bhutan
 d) India

5. Which Shakespearean character was safe until Birnam Wood came to Dunsinane Castle?
 a) Shylock
 b) Romeo
 c) Macbeth
 d) Orlando

6. In which film did Amitabh Bachchan do his own playback singing for the first time?
 a) *Mr Natwarlal*
 b) *Amar Akbar Anthony*
 c) *Baghban*
 d) *Kaalia*

7. Butterflies taste with their . . .
 a) Eyes
 b) Feet

c) Antennae

d) Heart

8. Which actress won the National Award for Best Actress three years in a row, for *Arth, Khandhar* and *Paar*?

a) Rakhee Gulzar

b) Sharmila Tagore

c) Smita Patil

d) Shabana Azmi

9. Which Belgian detective made his last appearance in the book *Curtain*?

a) Miss Marple

b) Sherlock Holmes

c) Father Brown

d) Hercule Poirot

10. The Roman *Acta Diurna*, appearing in 59 BCE, was the earliest recorded form of a . . .

a) Birth certificate

b) Quiz book

c) Calendar

d) Newspaper

11. With which well-known musician would you associate the book *My Music, My Life*?

a) Pandit Ravi Shankar

b) Shiv Kumar Sharma

c) Hariprasad Chaurasia

d) Bismillah Khan

12. The first Indian Institute of Technology, in Kharagpur, was built on the site of . . .
a) A British prison camp
b) Siraj-ud-Daulah's palace
c) Lord Clive's residence
d) A football stadium

13. On which famous ship did Lord Nelson die after being victorious at the Battle of Trafalgar?
a) *Endeavour*
b) *Santa Maria*
c) *Victory*
d) *Mayflower*

14. In 1863, cartoonist Thomas Nast was the first to paint whose definitive portrait?
a) Santa Claus
b) Shivaji
c) Queen Victoria
d) Mickey Mouse

15. Tamasha is a traditional folk theatre form of . . .
a) Tamil Nadu
b) Maharashtra
c) Uttar Pradesh
d) Gujarat

16. Which spice consists of the seeds of *Myristica fragrans*, a tropical evergreen tree?
a) Cumin
b) Nutmeg

c) Cardamom
d) Mustard

17. Which famous work by Vishnu Sharma was written to instruct the three dull princes of King Amarkirti of Mahilaranya?
a) *Panchatantra*
b) The Arthashastra
c) The Natyashastra
d) Rig Veda

18. What are you most likely to buy using the D–Z colour grading scale?
a) Mango
b) Diamond
c) Silk
d) Nail Polish

19. What were sometimes called 'dissected maps' and used to teach geography in eighteenth-century England?
a) Jigsaw puzzles
b) Monopoly
c) Tangrams
d) Crossword puzzles

20. Which martyr wrote under the pseudonym Balwant Singh?
a) Batukeshwar Dutt
b) Lala Lajpat Rai
c) Chandrasekhar Azad
d) Bhagat Singh

MOUNTAINS AND HILLS

1. Mount Everest is named after ...
   a) Sir George Everest, the then surveyor general of India
   b) The Greek god of mountains
   c) Edmund Hillary's nickname, 'Everest'
   d) After Lord John Henry Everest, viceroy of Nepal

2. Which mountain has three principal extinct volcanoes: Kibo, Mawenzi and Shira?
   a) Aconcagua
   b) Elbrus
   c) Kilimanjaro
   d) Fuji

3. Lake Kawaguchi is noted for reflecting the image of which mountain in its waters?
   a) Elbrus
   b) Kilimanjaro

c) Etna

d) Fuji

4. Which mountain system is often referred to as the spine of South America?
   a) Etna
   b) Andes
   c) Matterhorn
   d) Rocky

5. In Hindu mythology, who lifted the Govardhana mountain to save the people?
   a) Krishna
   b) Bhima
   c) Karna
   d) Duryodhana

6. What did Tenzing Norgay and Edmund Hillary leave behind on Mount Everest as an offering?
   a) Pens
   b) Tandoori chicken
   c) Oxygen cylinders
   d) Sweets

7. Which mountain range is divided into the Sambhar-Sirohi and Sambhar-Khetri ranges?
   a) Aravalli
   b) Satpura
   c) Himalayas
   d) Karakoram

8. Which little girl lived with her grandfather high in the Swiss Alps?
   a) Alice
   b) Anne Frank
   c) Heidi
   d) Lorna Doone

9. Which landmark is located on a hill called Neelachal Parbat, or Kamagiri, in Guwahati?
   a) Gol Gumbaz
   b) Kamakhya Temple
   c) Golden Temple
   d) Golconda Fort

10. In which continent are the 'eight-thousanders', the fourteen mountains that are higher than 8000 metres, located?
   a) Africa
   b) Asia
   c) South America
   d) Europe

11. The name of which mountain in Sikkim means 'five treasures of the great snow'?
   a) Kanchenjunga
   b) Mount Everest
   c) Lhotse
   d) K2

12. Name the most northerly pass that connects Pakistan and Afghanistan.
   a) Banihal Pass

b) Nathu La
c) Khyber Pass
d) Rohtang Pass

13. *Tiger of the Snows*, written in collaboration with James Ullman, is an autobiography of . . .
a) Tenzing Norgay
b) Reinhold Messner
c) George Mallory
d) Sir Edmund Hillary

14. Which of these is the largest volcano on earth?
a) Mount Rainier
b) Mauna Loa
c) Mount Etna
d) Mont Blanc

15. In which state would you come across the Baba Budan range, named after a saint who brought the first coffee seeds to India from Yemen?
a) Assam
b) Tamil Nadu
c) Karnataka
d) Haryana

16. What did Gutzon Borglum and his son Lincoln leave behind in the Black Hills of South Dakota, USA?
a) The carved heads of four US Presidents
b) Statues called moai
c) The Terracotta Army
d) Hoover Dam

17. K2, the world's second-highest peak, is part of which mountain range?
a) The Rockies
b) The Karakoram
c) The Vindhya Range
d) The Andes

18. The name of which mountain peak in Tamil Nadu literally means 'big mountain' in the Badaga language?
a) Anamudi
b) Mullayanagiri
c) Angida peak
d) Doddabetta

19. Mount Ararat is the highest point of which country?
a) China
b) Turkey
c) Sweden
d) Spain

20. Which is the highest battlefield in the world?
a) Garo Hills
b) Mount Aconcagua
c) Siachen Glacier
d) Napa Valley

MUGHALS

1. For which monument were 20,000 workmen accommodated in a small town named Mumtazabad in the 1630s?
    a) Red Fort
    b) Taj Mahal
    c) Agra Fort
    d) Purana Qila

2. Which Mughal emperor, the son of Shah Jahan, called himself Alamgir ('world conqueror')?
    a) Humayun
    b) Bahadur Shah
    c) Jahangir
    d) Aurangzeb

3. How was Nur Jahan related to Mumtaz Mahal?
    a) Nur Jahan and Mumtaz Mahal were sisters.
    b) Nur Jahan was Mumtaz Mahal's mother.

c) Nur Jahan was Mumtaz Mahal's aunt.

d) Nur Jahan was Mumtaz Mahal's grandmother.

4. Bahadur Shah II wrote poetry under the pen name . . .
   a) Ghalib
   b) Zauq
   c) Rumi
   d) Zafar

5. Jahangir built Shalimar Bagh for his wife. Name her.
   a) Jodha Bai
   b) Mumtaz Mahal
   c) Nur Jahan
   d) Anarkali

6. Akbar was born in Umarkot in 1542. In which present-day country is Umarkot located?
   a) Afghanistan
   b) Pakistan
   c) Uzbekistan
   d) Nepal

7. Who spent his last days looking at the Taj Mahal from Musamman Burj?
   a) Akbar
   b) Aurangzeb
   c) Humayun
   d) Shah Jahan

8. Which Mughal ruler introduced the *mansabdari* system in India?
   a) Akbar
   b) Babur
   c) Humayun
   d) Aurangzeb

9. After the mutiny of 1857, Bahadur Shah Zafar was exiled to ...
   a) Nepal
   b) Myanmar
   c) Sri Lanka
   d) Bhutan

10. His real name was Mahesh Das. His pen name was Brahma. Who was he?
   a) Birbal
   b) Tenali Raman
   c) Tansen
   d) Man Singh

11. When his son was unwell, this Mughal emperor is said to have offered his own life to God in exchange for his son's, walking around the bed seven times to complete the vow. Name him.
   a) Akbar
   b) Babur
   c) Humayun
   d) Jahangir

12. Who is said to have popularized chikankari in India?
   a) Nur Jahan
   b) Jodha Bai

c) Roshanara Begum

d) Anarkali

13. From which historical monument did Nadir Shah take the Peacock Throne?
    a) Purana Qila
    b) Taj Mahal
    c) Agra Fort
    d) Red Fort

14. Who defeated Humayun at the Battle of Chausa in 1539?
    a) Sher Shah Suri
    b) Mahmood Lodhi
    c) Maharana Pratap
    d) Rana Sanga

15. Name Akbar's revenue minister who had also served as Sher Shah's military engineer.
    a) Faizi
    b) Abul Fazal
    c) Man Singh
    d) Todar Mal

16. In 1569, whom did Haji Begum build a tomb for?
    a) Humayun
    b) Babur
    c) Akbar
    d) Jahangir

17. Which Mughal emperor was Jahangir's great-grandfather?
a) Babur
b) Humayun
c) Akbar
d) Shah Jahan

18. In which state is the historical city of Fatehpur Sikri located?
a) Uttar Pradesh
b) Haryana
c) Bihar
d) Maharashtra

19. What was constructed by Emperor Akbar on the remains of an ancient site known as Badalgarh?
a) Humayun's tomb
b) Red Fort
c) Agra Fort
d) Purana Qila

20. Which Mughal emperor was nicknamed Khurram?
a) Shah Jahan
b) Jahangir
c) Akbar
d) Babur

MUSIC

1. Whom did George Harrison call 'the godfather of world music'?
   a) Bismillah Khan
   b) Ravi Shankar
   c) Amjad Ali Khan
   d) Zakir Hussain

2. Which of these is a percussion instrument?
   a) Sitar
   b) Sarangi
   c) Shehnai
   d) Ghatam

3. Why would a musician use a plectrum?
   a) To carry his musical instrument
   b) To pluck the strings of his musical instrument

c) To rest his instrument on it

d) To hold the strings of the musical instrument in place

4. Who composed the music for the 1969 film *Goopy Gyne Bagha Byne*?

a) Ravi Shankar

b) Rabi Ghosh

c) Satyajit Ray

d) Kishore Kumar

5. In 1988, who became the youngest percussionist to be awarded the Padma Shri?

a) Zakir Hussain

b) Sivamani

c) Jnan Prakash Ghosh

d) Taufiq Qureshi

6. Which musical instrument is generally associated with Guru Nanak's friend and companion Mardana?

a) Dholak

b) Tanpura

c) Rebab

d) Santoor

7. Who received the Bharat Ratna in 2001, along with Bismillah Khan?

a) Lata Mangeshkar

b) Ravi Shankar

c) Asha Bhosle

d) M.S. Subbulakshmi

8. Which musical instrument was referred to as the *shata-tantri veena* in ancient times?
- a) Santoor
- b) Tanpura
- c) Tar Shehnai
- d) Ektara

9. Guitarist Syd Barrett helped found which rock band that was named after two famous blues musicians?
- a) Led Zeppelin
- b) Guns N' Roses
- c) Queen
- d) Pink Floyd

10. Which of these words describes the sound made by an elephant as well as a musical instrument?
- a) Trombone
- b) Trumpet
- c) Saxophone
- d) Tuba

11. Howie, AJ, Kevin, Brian and Nick formed the group . . .
- a) Backstreet Boys
- b) Boyzone
- c) NSYNC
- d) Wham!

12. Which musical instrument is also known as *venu, vamsi, murali, pillankarovi* and *kolalu*?
- a) Flute
- b) Violin

c) Sitar

d) Guitar

13. In Indian music, what is the term used for the first line of a song or composition?

a) *Sargam*

b) *Taal*

c) *Antara*

d) *Mukhda*

14. The name of which Indian percussion instrument literally means 'made of clay'?

a) Mridangam

b) Shehnai

c) Santoor

d) Veena

15. Who was the first Indian female singer to receive the Ramon Magsaysay Award?

a) Lata Mangeshkar

b) M.S. Subbulakshmi

c) Asha Bhosle

d) Kishori Amonkar

16. *Moonwalk* is the autobiography of . . .

a) Michael Jackson

b) John Lennon

c) Madonna

d) Phil Collins

17. Who, along with Hariprasad Chaurasia, composed music for the films *Chandni* and *Silsila*?
   a) Shiv Kumar Sharma
   b) Zakir Hussain
   c) Bismillah Khan
   d) Amjad Ali Khan

18. How is Abhas Kumar Ganguly better known?
   a) Kumar Sanu
   b) Kishore Kumar
   c) Shaan
   d) Abhijeet

19. Ringo Starr, John Lennon and George Harrison were all members of the Beatles. Who was the fourth member?
   a) Paul McCartney
   b) Art Garfunkel
   c) Ray Charles
   d) Bob Dylan

20. Who composed a number of songs and plays under the pen name Akhtari Pia?
   a) Wajid Ali Shah
   b) Tansen
   c) Akbar
   d) Rabindranath Tagore

ORGANIZATIONS

1. 'Duty unto death' is the motto of which organization in India?
   a) Indian Police Service
   b) Border Security Force
   c) Rapid Action Force
   d) Indian Coast Guard

2. Which of these organizations began in 1971 and was then called the Don't Make a Wave Committee?
   a) The Nature Conservancy
   b) WWF
   c) Greenpeace
   d) Conservation International

3. In India, which branch of the Ministry of Defence was set up as an armed force of the Union in 1978 on recommendations from the Rustamji Committee?
   a) Central Reserve Police Force

b) National Disaster Response Force
c) Indian Coast Guard
d) Indo-Tibetan Border Police

4. Which colour forms the background of the UN's flag?
a) Red
b) Blue
c) Yellow
d) Green

5. OPEC is a multinational organization that coordinates policies related to . . .
a) Oilseeds
b) Petroleum
c) Electronics
d) Construction

6. Rudolf Diels was the first head of the organization initially called Department 1A of the Prussian State Police. Later it came to be known as . . .
a) The CIA
b) The KGB
c) The Gestapo
d) INTERPOL

7. The logo of which organization features a burning candle wrapped in barbed wire?
a) Amnesty International
b) Missionaries of Charity
c) World Health Organization
d) People for the Ethical Treatment of Animals

8. In which city are the headquarters of the United Nations located?
   a) New York City
   b) The Hague
   c) Geneva
   d) Moscow

9. The PIN code starting with the digit 9 is reserved for . . .
   a) The Indian Army
   b) Red Cross
   c) Parliament House
   d) The Indian Space Research Organization (ISRO)

10. The five rings that appear on the Olympic flag represent . . .
   a) The five original events in the modern Olympic Games
   b) The five colours on the coat of arms of Greece
   c) The five continents joined in the Olympic Movement
   d) The five elements

11. In India, Public Service Broadcasting Day is celebrated on 12 November to commemorate whose visit to the All India Radio broadcasting station?
   a) Mahatma Gandhi
   b) Jawaharlal Nehru
   c) Subhas Chandra Bose
   d) Rajendra Prasad

12. Why was 'Be prepared' chosen as the motto for the Boy Scouts movement?
   a) They were Baden-Powell's favourite two words.
   b) For no reason, just for kicks

c) It also stood for the initials (BP) of its founder.
d) None of the above

13. What started its first commercial service on 16 April 1853?
    a) Indian Railways
    b) Airports Authority of India
    c) Indian Armed Forces
    d) India Post

14. *Hum Sab Bharatiya Hain* is the song of . . .
    a) The Film and Television Institute of India
    b) The National Cadet Corps
    c) The National School of Drama
    d) The National Security Guard

15. Which secretary general of the United Nations won the Nobel Peace Prize in 2001?
    a) Boutros Boutros-Ghali
    b) Kofi Annan
    c) Javier Pérez de Cuéllar
    d) Ban Ki-moon

16. Which of these animals has been a part of WWF's logo since its founding in 1961?
    a) Giant panda
    b) Koala
    c) Red kangaroo
    d) Musk deer

17. Before Independence, it was the Crown Representative's Police. How do we know it today?
   a) CBI
   b) BSF
   c) CRPF
   d) NCC

18. At the end of which war was the League of Nations formed?
   a) World War I
   b) World War II
   c) The Wars of the Roses
   d) The Crimean War

19. The Federal Bureau of Investigation (FBI) is the principal investigative agency of ...
   a) The USA
   b) The UK
   c) France
   d) Germany

20. Which country won the first competition organized by the Fédération Internationale de Football Association (FIFA)?
   a) Argentina
   b) Uruguay
   c) Italy
   d) Spain

PHYSICS

1. The tungsten filament in a light bulb does not burn because …
   a) It is not heated.
   b) It is coated with iron.
   c) It is incombustible.
   d) It is in a sealed, oxygen-free chamber.

2. If you were living in Srinagar and snowfall blocked your door, which common condiment would you use to unblock it?
   a) Salt
   b) Sugar
   c) Pepper
   d) Chilli flakes

3. Which instrument is used to measure the speed of airflow in the atmosphere?
   a) Barometer
   b) Chronometer

c) Odometer
d) Anemometer

4. In 1798, Nicolas-Louis Robert invented the first machine to produce what in continuous sheets?
a) Fibre glass
b) Steel
c) Paper
d) Cotton cloth

5. What did Sir Percy L. Spencer invent following the accidental melting of a bar of chocolate?
a) Pressure cooker
b) Microwave oven
c) Refrigerator
d) Vacuum cleaner

6. According to Newton's third law of motion, every action has ...
a) A rotational motion
b) An equal and opposite reaction
c) A reaction in the same direction
d) A reaction with a higher force

7. The change between the solid and the gaseous phases of matter, with no intermediate liquid stage, is known as ...
a) Vaporization
b) Evaporation
c) Condensation
d) Sublimation

8. A positive charge is developed in a body when it ...
a) Gains neutrons
b) Gains electrons
c) Loses protons
d) Loses electrons

9. A set of rules to be followed in problem-solving operations, especially by a computer, is called ...
a) Algorithm
b) Calculus
c) Mensuration
d) Trigonometry

10. What is the temperature at which Fahrenheit and Celsius scales show the same numeric value?
a) –20 degrees
b) –40 degrees
c) 0 degree
d) 100 degrees

11. The steam engine, invented by James Watt, was initially used for ...
a) Ironing clothes
b) Pumping water
c) Mowing grass
d) Boiling potatoes

12. An ordinary triangular prism can separate white light into its constituent colours, called the ...
a) Aurora borealis
b) Spectrum

c) Shadow
d) Mirage

13. What does the Mohs scale measure?
a) Density of a substance
b) Velocity
c) Hardness of minerals
d) Ductility of a metal

14. Which rhyme did Thomas Alva Edison use to test his phonograph?
a) 'Baa Baa Black Sheep'
b) 'Twinkle Twinkle Little Star'
c) 'Mary Had a Little Lamb'
d) 'Johnny Johnny'

15. Tides are caused due to the gravitational pull of . . .
a) Comets
b) Meteors
c) The sun
d) The moon

16. _____: A Biography of the World's Most Famous Equation. Fill in the blank to complete the name of a book by David Bodanis.
a) p=mv
b) E=mc^2
c) a^2+b^2=c^2
d) F-E+V=2

17. Who among these artists is credited with designing a revolving crane, a pulley, a lagoon dredge and a flying ship?
   a) Pablo Picasso
   b) Leonardo da Vinci
   c) Salvador Dali
   d) Vincent van Gogh

18. In physics, what would the mass of an object multiplied by its velocity give you?
   a) Acceleration
   b) Kinetic energy
   c) Gravitational force
   d) Momentum

19. Which of these instruments is used to measure electric current?
   a) Ammeter
   b) Odometer
   c) Anemometer
   d) Barometer

20. Fill in the blank: The wheel and axle, the lever, the ramp, the screw and the pulley are all _____ machines.
   a) Normal
   b) Complex
   c) Complicated
   d) Simple

PLANTS AND TREES

1. Which tree is sometimes referred to as the 'village pharmacy' because of its numerous health benefits?
   a) Banyan
   b) Neem
   c) Peepul
   d) Sandalwood

2. A certain species of which plant is the fastest-growing plant on earth?
   a) Banana
   b) Bamboo
   c) Hemp
   d) Rubber

3. What is the state tree of Karnataka?
   a) Sal
   b) Teak

c) Sandalwood

d) Neem

4. What is obtained from the bark of the cinchona tree and is used chiefly in the treatment of malaria?
a) Cinnamon
b) Quinine
c) Vanilla
d) Mohair

5. What do we know the rhizome of the plant *Zingiber officinale* as?
a) Ginger
b) Garlic
c) Bamboo
d) Asparagus

6. The most expensive spice in the world is derived from the dry stigmata of the plants. We popularly know it as . . .
a) Mace
b) Turmeric
c) Saffron
d) Cinnamon

7. *Hevea brasiliensis* is the scientific name of the . . .
a) Teak tree
b) Rubber tree
c) Mulberry tree
d) Eucalyptus tree

8. Which of these is a coarse fibre obtained from the outer shells of coconuts?
   a) Flax
   b) Jute
   c) Hemp
   d) Coir

9. Which variety of mango is named after the second Governor of sixteenth-century Portuguese India, A. de Albuquerque?
   a) Langra
   b) Alphonso
   c) Zardalu
   d) Himsagar

10. Koalas feed primarily on the leaves of which plant?
   a) Teak
   b) Eucalyptus
   c) Bamboo
   d) Acacia

11. Which of these is also known as the 'golden fibre'?
   a) Jute
   b) Flax
   c) Cotton
   d) Ramie

12. *Oryza sativa* is the scientific name of which annual grass?
   a) Rice
   b) Wheat
   c) Maize
   d) Barley

13. What is obtained from the plant *Camellia sinensis*?
a) Coffee
b) Tea
c) Turmeric
d) Pepper

14. Flax fibres, obtained from the stems of the plant *Linum usitatissimum*, are mainly used to make . . .
a) Jute
b) Cotton
c) Linen
d) Silk

15. Thompson Seedless, Sonaka and Anab-e-Shahi are the major Indian varieties of which fruit?
a) Lemon
b) Watermelon
c) Grape
d) Cranberry

16. *Ficus religiosa* is the scientific name of the . . .
a) Banyan tree
b) Peepul tree
c) Tulsi plant
d) Neem tree

17. An individual banana is referred to by the same term as which part of the human body?
a) The finger
b) The toe

c) The ear
d) The eye

18. The name of which spice comes from the French word for 'nail'?
a) Cinnamon
b) Cardamom
c) Clove
d) Cumin

19. From which part of the plant is cinnamon obtained?
a) Root
b) Leaf
c) Inner bark
d) Flower

20. The name of which of these trees comes from a Malayalam or Tamil word?
a) Peepul
b) Teak
c) Banyan
d) Sal

POLITICS

1. In the Lok Sabha, which state has the highest number of seats?
   a) Maharashtra
   b) Uttar Pradesh
   c) West Bengal
   d) Karnataka

2. Which was the first country in the world to grant national voting rights to women?
   a) The USA
   b) New Zealand
   c) Spain
   d) The UK

3. If the President of India wishes to resign from their post, they need to address the letter of resignation to the . . .
   a) Vice president
   b) Prime minister

c) Minister of defence
d) Minister of home affairs

4. Which phrase is used to describe a prime minister's inner cabinet, or most trusted members?
   a) Bedroom cabinet
   b) Shadow cabinet
   c) Dining cabinet
   d) Kitchen cabinet

5. While doing a census in an Indian state, whose name is listed first?
   a) The chief minister
   b) The oldest resident
   c) The police commissioner
   d) The Governor

6. What was adopted on 26 November 1949 but came into force on 26 January 1950?
   a) The Constitution of India
   b) The national flag
   c) The national emblem
   d) The national anthem

7. Which was the first country to gain independence in the present millennium?
   a) Kosovo
   b) East Timor
   c) Palau
   d) Eritrea

8. Who among these advises the Government of India on legal matters?
   a) The attorney general
   b) The speaker of the Lok Sabha
   c) The minister of human resource development
   d) The vice president

9. Sri Jayawardenepura Kotte is the legislative and judicial capital of . . .
   a) The Maldives
   b) Sri Lanka
   c) The Seychelles
   d) Malaysia

10. What fraction of the Rajya Sabha retires every second year?
    a) Half
    b) One-third
    c) One-fourth
    d) Two-third

11. In India, who heads the Department of Space as a cabinet minister?
    a) The President
    b) The prime minister
    c) The minister of defence
    d) The minister of finance

12. What is the London address of Britain's chancellor of the exchequer?
    a) 11 Downing Street
    b) 221B Baker Street

c) 4 Privet Drive
d) 32 Windsor Gardens

13. In India, what does Mysore Paints and Varnish Ltd provide during an election?
a) Ballot boxes
b) Indelible ink
c) Electronic voting machines
d) The electoral roll

14. What was founded at the Gokuldas Tejpal Sanskrit Pathshala?
a) The Communist Party of India (Marxist)
b) The All India Forward Bloc
c) The Bharatiya Janata Party
d) The Indian National Congress

15. In the 1984 general election, who defeated Hemwati Nandan Bahuguna from Allahabad?
a) Rajiv Gandhi
b) Amitabh Bachchan
c) Milkha Singh
d) M.F. Husain

16. Who was the only finance minister to have had the opportunity to present two budgets on his birthday—in 1964 and again in 1968?
a) Morarji Desai
b) S.B. Chavan
c) Pranab Mukherjee
d) T.T. Krishnamachari

17. What is the first hour of every sitting of the Lok Sabha called?
a) Question Hour
b) Business Hour
c) Discussion Hour
d) Zero Hour

18. Which is the only Union Territory to have a high court of its own?
a) Puducherry
b) Chandigarh
c) Delhi
d) Lakshadweep

19. Who is the ex-officio chairman of the Rajya Sabha?
a) The President
b) The vice president
c) The prime minister of India
d) The chief justice of India

20. The formal workplace of the President of the United States is called the . . .
a) Oval Office
b) Pentagon
c) Capitol Hill
d) Chrysler Building

SCIENTISTS

1. Who was the first national professor of independent India?
   a) Satyendra Nath Bose
   b) C.V. Raman
   c) Jagadish Chandra Bose
   d) Prasanta Chandra Mahalanobis

2. Which scientist was offered the presidency of Israel after Chaim Weizmann's death in 1952?
   a) Julius Robert Oppenheimer
   b) Albert Einstein
   c) Niels Bohr
   d) Thomas Alva Edison

3. He was an American artist known for his dot-and-dash code system. Identify him.
   a) Van Gogh
   b) Louis Braille

   c)   Alexander Graham Bell
   d)   Samuel Morse

4. Which useful mathematical tool is John Napier's most famous invention?
   a)   Abacus
   b)   Calculator
   c)   Logarithms
   d)   Slide rule

5. Who saved the beer and silk industries in France and developed vaccines against anthrax and rabies?
   a)   Alexander Fleming
   b)   Alfred Nobel
   c)   Joseph Priestly
   d)   Louis Pasteur

6. Which of these chemical elements is not named after an inventor?
   a)   Einsteinium
   b)   Ruthenium
   c)   Nobelium
   d)   Fermium

7. The laboratory notebooks of which duo were checked for radiation before being auctioned in 1984?
   a)   Carl and Gerty Cori
   b)   William Henry and William Lawrence Bragg
   c)   Frederic and Irene Joliot-Curie
   d)   Pierre and Marie Curie

8. Who was appointed warden of the Royal Mint of the UK in 1696?
   a) Isaac Newton
   b) Galileo Galilei
   c) Francis Bacon
   d) Charles Darwin

9. Whose first patented invention was the electrical vote recorder?
   a) Guglielmo Marconi
   b) Thomas Alva Edison
   c) Edwin Hubble
   d) Robert Boyle

10. After which scientist was the third member of the Great Observatory family of NASA named?
    a) Johannes Kepler
    b) William Herschel
    c) Carl Sagan
    d) Subrahmanyan Chandrasekhar

11. Which famous scientist, born in 1893, was a member of the first Lok Sabha from West Bengal?
    a) Meghnad Saha
    b) Satyendra Nath Bose
    c) Prafulla Chandra Ray
    d) Jagadish Chandra Bose

12. Whom did C.V. Raman refer to as 'the modern equivalent of Leonardo da Vinci'?
    a) Birbal Sahni

b) Homi Bhabha
c) Vikram Sarabhai
d) Shanti Swaroop Bhatnagar

13. Which scientist coined the name 'oxygen'?
a) Antoine Lavoisier
b) Daniel Rutherford
c) John Dalton
d) Robert Boyle

14. With which invention would you associate the words 'Mr Watson, come here—I want to see you'?
a) Printing press
b) Telephone
c) Sewing machine
d) Telegraph

15. In 1929, Alexander Fleming published the discovery of which of the following in the *British Journal of Experimental Pathology*?
a) Blood groups
b) Penicillin
c) Nitrogen
d) Structure of DNA

16. Which chemist is best known for his contributions to the discovery of chlorine as well as iodine and for his invention of a device that improved the safety of coal miners?
a) Christian Doppler
b) Louis Pasteur
c) Humphry Davy
d) Benjamin Franklin

17. Who is credited with the invention of bifocals?
   a) Benjamin Franklin
   b) Leonardo da Vinci
   c) Galileo Galilei
   d) Nicolaus Copernicus

18. Fill in the blank to complete this quote by Albert Einstein: '_____ is more difficult than physics.'
   a) Philosophy
   b) Journalism
   c) Politics
   d) Literature

19. Why didn't Alexander Graham Bell's mother and wife use the telephone he invented?
   a) They were both deaf.
   b) Both had died before it was invented.
   c) Both hated machines.
   d) He was divorced, and his mother was dead.

20. Dr U.N. Brahmachari used urea stibamine to successfully treat which disease?
   a) Kala-azar
   b) Malaria
   c) Typhoid
   d) Cholera

SPORTS

1. Whose birth anniversary is celebrated as National Sports Day in India?
   a) Milkha Singh
   b) Dhyan Chand
   c) Ranjitsinhji
   d) K.D. Jadhav

2. In 1982, the ninth Asian Games in New Delhi coincided with . . .
   a) The inauguration of the Lotus Temple
   b) The advent of colour television in India
   c) The first Filmfare Awards
   d) Indira Gandhi's death

3. Whose autobiography is titled *Golden Girl*?
   a) Steffi Graf
   b) P.T. Usha

c) Nadia Comăneci

d) Jackie Joyner-Kersee

4. In Japanese, the name of which martial art form literally means 'empty hand'?
   a) Taekwondo
   b) Aikido
   c) Kung fu
   d) Karate

5. My father was a hockey Olympian. My mother was a basketball player of repute. I, too, am a famous Indian sportsman. Who am I?
   a) Leander Paes
   b) Prakash Padukone
   c) Pankaj Advani
   d) Vishwanathan Anand

6. There are two very common ways of holding a table tennis bat. If one is the shakehand grip, which is the other?
   a) Penhold grip
   b) Fist grip
   c) Chopstick grip
   d) Button grip

7. Which game is often called the Hungarian Horror?
   a) Scrabble
   b) Rubik's Cube
   c) Chess
   d) Monopoly

8. With which sport would you associate the jumping style called Fosbury Flop?
   a) Long jump
   b) High jump
   c) Pole vault
   d) Triple jump

9. What sport would you be good at if you represented your school at the Subroto Cup?
   a) Football
   b) Hockey
   c) Tennis
   d) Badminton

10. Why was champion swimmer Dawn Fraser banned from competitions for many years?
   a) She allegedly stole a flag from the Japanese Imperial Palace.
   b) She tested positive for drugs.
   c) He was a man participating as a woman.
   d) She burnt a kimono in public.

11. A winner in which sport receives the Venus Rosewater Dish?
   a) Tennis
   b) Swimming
   c) Boxing
   d) Badminton

12. Which was the first sporting event to be telecast live on television?
   a) The first Asian Games

b) The 1930 FIFA World Cup
c) The 1940 Wimbledon Championships
d) The 1936 Berlin Olympics

13. Which sportsman was nicknamed Louisville Lip because of the way he used to boast before a contest?
a) Pelé
b) Maradona
c) Muhammad Ali
d) Jimmy Connors

14. Which famous game was invented by James Naismith in 1891 to help his students keep fit during winter?
a) Basketball
b) Badminton
c) Squash
d) Table tennis

15. The name of which sport has been attributed to a French word meaning 'shepherd's crook'?
a) Cricket
b) Hockey
c) Golf
d) Polo

16. Fifty-five-year-old Bobby Riggs lost against which female tennis star in a challenge match in the mid-seventies?
a) Martina Navratilova
b) Chris Evert
c) Margaret Court
d) Billie Jean King

17. Which of these is known as 'suicide in ten instalments'?
   a) Boxing
   b) Polo
   c) Decathlon
   d) Archery

18. Which of these sports is played with three variations—on horse, cycle and elephant?
   a) Boxing
   b) Polo
   c) Weightlifting
   d) Snooker

19. In which sport would the Boston Celtics compete against the Chicago Bulls?
   a) Basketball
   b) Baseball
   c) Volleyball
   d) Football

20. What reason did King Edward III give for banning football in 1365?
   a) The soldiers were not concentrating on archery.
   b) The ball was causing a lot of injuries to players.
   c) The king wanted only the royals to play the game.
   d) The ball was very expensive.

SUPERLATIVES

1. Who was the first woman to feature on an Indian stamp?
   a) Indira Gandhi
   b) Mira Bai
   c) Lakshmibai
   d) Mother Teresa

2. Which monument, with a diameter of 14.32 metres at the base and about 2.75 metres on the top, has a height of 72.5 metres?
   a) Charminar
   b) Qutub Minar
   c) Buland Darwaza
   d) India Gate

3. Which bird lays the largest eggs in the world in proportion to its body size?
   a) Ostrich

b) Emu

c) Sarus crane

d) Kiwi

4. Who was the first American author to submit a typewritten manuscript?
   a) Mark Twain
   b) Nathaniel Hawthorne
   c) Ernest Hemingway
   d) Herman Melville

5. The highest point on earth is called Sagarmatha in Nepali and Chomolungma in Tibetan. How do we commonly know it?
   a) Mount Everest
   b) Kanchenjunga
   c) Mount Godwin-Austen
   d) Nanga Parbat

6. Sushmita Sen became Miss Universe in 1994. Who was crowned Miss World that year?
   a) Lara Dutta
   b) Reita Faria
   c) Diana Hayden
   d) Aishwarya Rai

7. According to the 2011 census of India, Rajasthan is the . . .
   a) First e-literate state in India
   b) First state to ban plastic
   c) Largest state in terms of area
   d) Only state to have lions in the wild

8. What is the name of the oldest surviving functional steam engine in the world?
   a) Fairy Queen
   b) My Fair Lady
   c) Sweet Caroline
   d) Black Beauty

9. In 2011, who entered the Guinness World Records for the highest number of single studio recordings?
   a) Lata Mangeshkar
   b) Asha Bhosle
   c) Kumar Sanu
   d) Alka Yagnik

10. Which continent has the largest desert and the longest river in the world?
   a) Africa
   b) South America
   c) Asia
   d) Europe

11. Who became the first woman member of the Royal Statistical Society in 1858 because of her contribution to army statistics?
   a) Marie Curie
   b) Amelia Earhart
   c) Valentina Tereshkova
   d) Florence Nightingale

12. Which is the oldest existing freshwater lake on earth?
   a) Baikal
   b) Huron

c) Superior

d) Titicaca

13. Junko Tabei was the first woman to . . .
   a) Win the Nobel Prize
   b) Climb Mount Everest
   c) Reach the South Pole
   d) Swim across the English Channel

14. Who was the first Indian to enter the Indian Civil Service?
   a) Satyendranath Tagore
   b) Surendranath Banerjee
   c) Sukumar Sen
   d) Satyendra Nath Bose

15. The largest drainage system in the world in terms of volume is . . .
   a) Ganga
   b) Nile
   c) Mississippi
   d) Amazon

16. Who is the only person to have been awarded two unshared Nobel Prizes?
   a) Frederick Sanger
   b) Marie Curie
   c) Linus Pauling
   d) Roger D. Kornberg

17. The Howrah–Amritsar Express has the most number of . . .
   a) Bogies
   b) Stops

c) Staff

d) Railroad switches

18. Which metal has the highest electrical conductivity of all metals?
    a) Gold
    b) Silver
    c) Platinum
    d) Cobalt

19. On whose life is the 1977 film *The Greatest* based?
    a) Marilyn Monroe
    b) Muhammad Ali
    c) Elvis Presley
    d) John F. Kennedy

20. Which of these places is recognized by the Guinness World Records as 'the wettest place on earth'?
    a) Haflong
    b) Mawsynram
    c) Wokha
    d) Cherrapunji

THE GREAT EPICS I

1. In the Ramayana, what name did Nemi receive because his chariot could move in ten different directions at the same time?
    a) Ravana
    b) Dasharatha
    c) Kumbhakarna
    d) Bharata

2. Lord Krishna's Panchajanya is a . . .
    a) Bow
    b) Conch shell
    c) Mace
    d) Chakra

3. In the Ramayana, who used his Vajrayudha in order to prevent Hanuman from eating the sun?
    a) Indra

b) Vayu
c) Agni
d) Shiva

4. At birth, Duryodhana cried like a/an ...
   a) Ass
   b) Horse
   c) Elephant
   d) Lion

5. In the Ramayana, who received the title of Indrajit after he defeated Indra in a battle?
   a) Vibhishana
   b) Meghnad
   c) Kumbhakarna
   d) Ravana

6. Anusuya, Atri's wife, gave an ointment to a lady so that she could stay beautiful forever. Who was the lady?
   a) Shakuntala
   b) Mandavi
   c) Sita
   d) Kaikeyi

7. In the Ramayana, what was the name of the lady who took a bite of each fruit before she offered it to Rama?
   a) Ahalya
   b) Sabari
   c) Menaka
   d) Manthara

8. In the Mahabharata, who cursed Krishna that he would be killed by trickery?
a) Madri
b) Kunti
c) Draupadi
d) Gandhari

9. In the Ramayana, which rakshasa was known as Jaya and served as Vishnu's gatekeeper in Vaikuntha?
a) Mareecha
b) Subahu
c) Ravana
d) Hidimba

10. In the Ramayana, what was the name of Rama's sister?
a) Urmila
b) Kanta
c) Shanta
d) Dussala

11. In the Ramayana, who became the king of Kishkindha immediately after Bali's death?
a) Vibhishana
b) Hanuman
c) Jatayu
d) Sugriva

12. In the Mahabharata, which great sage was the spiritual teacher of the Pandavas and the Kauravas?
a) Kanva
b) Agastya

c) Valmiki
d) Veda Vyasa

13. In the Mahabharata, who taught Bhima the use of a mace?
a) Eklavya
b) Balarama
c) Karna
d) Krishna

14. Whom did Krishna defeat and take the Syamantaka jewel from?
a) Jatayu
b) Nala
c) Sugriva
d) Jambavan

15. In the Ramayana, what was the name of the chariot in which Ravana forcefully took Sita to Lanka?
a) Pushpaka Vimana
b) Hansa Yukta
c) Kalasha
d) Tripurajit

16. Wife of King Dasharatha, she was the mother of Bharata. Name her.
a) Kaushalya
b) Sumitra
c) Kaikeyi
d) Ahalya

17. What was the original name of the Mahabharata composed by Vyasa?
   a) Menaka
   b) Uttara
   c) Gita
   d) Jaya

18. In the Mahabharata, who killed Shakuni during the war?
   a) Karna
   b) Sahadeva
   c) Nakula
   d) Arjuna

19. Name the rakshasi who consoled Sita at Ashok Vatika.
   a) Trijata
   b) Ahalya
   c) Manthara
   d) Shakuntala

20. In the Mahabharata, which grandson of Pandu died in warfare when he was surrounded in a *chakravyuha*?
   a) Yaudheya
   b) Prativindhya
   c) Abhimanyu
   d) Ghatotkacha

THE GREAT EPICS II

1. In the Mahabharata, who was Dhritarashtra's only daughter by Gandhari?
   a) Mandavi
   b) Chitrangada
   c) Urvashi
   d) Dussala

2. Which famous sage inspired Valmiki to compose the Ramayana?
   a) Hanuman
   b) Narada
   c) Jambavan
   d) Jatayu

3. Who wrote the Mahabharata at Vyasa's dictation?
   a) Krishna
   b) Ganesha

c) Narada
d) Indra

4. In the Ramayana, who was the eldest son of Vishrava and Kaikasi?
a) Ravana
b) Vibhishana
c) Meghnad
d) Kumbhakarna

5. Shantanu had two wives. If one was Satyavati, who was the other?
a) Gandhari
b) Ambika
c) Ambalika
d) Ganga

6. In the Mahabharata, what profession did Arjuna take up at Raja Virata's court?
a) Palanquin bearer
b) Guard
c) Dance and music teacher
d) Cook

7. In the Ramayana, who accidentally killed Shravan Kumar?
a) Rama
b) Dasharatha
c) Bharata
d) Ravana

8. In the Mahabharata, who was Kunti's eldest son?
    a) Nakula
    b) Bhima
    c) Karna
    d) Duryodhana

9. In the Ramayana, whose wife was Srutakirti?
    a) Rama
    b) Bharata
    c) Lakshmana
    d) Shatrughna

10. In the Ramayana, who became the king of Lanka after Ravana
    was defeated and killed?
    a) Hidimba
    b) Kumbhakarna
    c) Indrajit
    d) Vibhishana

11. In the Mahabharata, which snake killed Parikshit?
    a) Kaliya
    b) Takshaka
    c) Vasuki
    d) Sheshanaga

12. In the Ramayana, which rakshasa took the form of a golden
    deer to lure Lakshmana away, leaving Sita unprotected?
    a) Mareecha
    b) Khara
    c) Tataka
    d) Mara

13. In the Mahabharata, who married the demoness Hidimbi?
  a) Nakul
  b) Arjuna
  c) Bhima
  d) Sahadeva

14. In the Mahabharata, who gave Parashuram an axe named Parashu?
  a) Vishnu
  b) Brahma
  c) Shiva
  d) His mother

15. The Bhagavad Gita is in the form of a conversation between Lord Krishna and . . .
  a) Arjuna
  b) Bhima
  c) Draupadi
  d) Madri

16. In the Ramayana, who lodged herself on Kumbhakarna's tongue and made him ask for the boon of sleep from Brahma?
  a) Saraswati
  b) Lakshmi
  c) Durga
  d) Kali

17. In the Mahabharata, who was also known as Gangeya?
  a) Karna
  b) Bhishma

c) Arjuna

d) Pandu

18. On being caught by this dacoit, the *saptarishi*s told him to ask
his family whether they would share his sins. When they said
no, this dacoit changed his ways. Who is being referred to?
a) Hanuman
b) Valmiki
c) Rama
d) Dasharatha

19. In the Mahabharata, which Pandava was also known as
Dhananjaya?
a) Yudhisthira
b) Arjuna
c) Nakula
d) Sahadeva

20. Who was the commander in general of the Pandava forces
during the battle of Kurukshetra?
a) Abhimanyu
b) Krishna
c) Sanjaya
d) Dhrishtadyumna

TRAVEL ACROSS INDIA

1. The land for which famous monument was acquired from the Kachhwahas of Ajmer in exchange for four havelis?
   a) Red Fort
   b) Taj Mahal
   c) Hawa Mahal
   d) Charminar

2. The Bada Imambara in Lucknow was built in 1784 as a . . .
   a) Prison .
   b) Tribute to Wajid Ali Shah
   c) Mausoleum for Aurangzeb
   d) Famine relief project

3. The Godan Express is named after a book by . . .
   a) Rabindranath Tagore
   b) Munshi Premchand

c) Sarat Chandra Chattopadhyay
d) Mahadevi Verma

4. In 1947, the last British regiment to leave India departed from ...
   a) Gateway of India
   b) Charminar
   c) Fort Kochi
   d) Victoria Memorial

5. Built in 1591, the Charminar was built to commemorate ...
   a) The beginning of Muhammad Quli Qutab Shah's rule
   b) The Battle of Bobbili
   c) The end of the plague
   d) The mystic queen Bhagmati's death

6. Which mode of transport was discontinued in Chennai on 11 April 1953?
   a) Trams
   b) Minibuses
   c) Horse-drawn carriages
   d) Cycle rickshaws

7. Which of these is said to be one of the reasons why Jaipur is called the Pink City?
   a) The world's largest pink roses are grown there.
   b) It was coloured pink for the Prince of Wales's (King Edward VII) visit in 1876.
   c) It was the third Maharana's daughter's favourite colour.
   d) It was originally painted red; then it rained.

8. In the complex of which tourist destination in Delhi would you find the famous Iron Pillar built in memory of a mighty king named Chandra?
a) Qutub Minar
b) Red Fort
c) Purana Qila
d) Humayun's Tomb

9. According to a story, the Hawa Mahal was designed to resemble . . .
a) Lord Krishna's crown
b) The moon
c) Mount Everest
d) A tabla

10. The Sun Temple in Konark is a representation of the Sun god Surya's . . .
a) Palace
b) Chariot
c) Conch shell
d) Feet

11. One of the principal seats of the Chandela rulers is a world heritage site. Name it.
a) Khajuraho
b) Mahabalipuram
c) Hampi
d) Ayodhya

12. In 1996, after which famous Indian was the Victoria Terminus renamed?
a) Chhatrapati Shivaji
b) Mahatma Gandhi
c) Subhas Chandra Bose
d) Indira Gandhi

13. In 1984, Rakesh Sharma went into space and Bachendri Pal became the first Indian woman to climb Mount Everest. What was launched for the first time in Calcutta, and indeed in India, on 24 October 1984?
a) The Calcutta Metro
b) Tram service
c) Autorickshaws
d) Double-decker buses

14. Which famous mausoleum was called 'a teardrop on the cheek of time' by Rabindranath Tagore?
a) Taj Mahal
b) Safdarjung's Tomb
c) Bibi ka Maqbara
d) Gol Gumbaz

15. Which landmark, designed by Fariborz Sabha, was dedicated in 1986?
a) Lotus Temple
b) Golden Temple
c) Victoria Memorial
d) Victoria Terminus

16. In which state is the Archaeological Museum of Sarnath located?
   a) Madhya Pradesh
   b) Uttar Pradesh
   c) Maharashtra
   d) Bihar

17. The roads of which Indian Union Territory are based on a unique plan called the '7 V's by its planner?
   a) Puducherry
   b) The Andaman and Nicobar Islands
   c) Chandigarh
   d) Daman and Diu

18. *Mahesa Murti* is one of the most famous sculptures of which landmark?
   a) Ajanta Caves
   b) Dilwara Temples
   c) Konark Sun Temple
   d) Elephanta Caves

19. Which landmark is also known as the All India War Memorial?
   a) India Gate
   b) Gateway of India
   c) Buland Darwaza
   d) Shaheed Minar

20. Name the place of worship that stands in the middle of Amrita Sarovar.
   a) Golden Temple
   b) Kamakhya Temple
   c) Jama Masjid
   d) Dilwara Temple

WARS AND BATTLES

1. What was the Gestapo?
   a) The German Secret State Police during World War II
   b) A submarine developed in Japan
   c) The site of a concentration camp in Poland
   d) A book by Karl Marx

2. Who defeated Darius III in the Battle of Gaugamela?
   a) Tamerlane
   b) Genghis Khan
   c) Alexander the Great
   d) Julius Caesar

3. In the 1800s, in which conflict did Britain, France, Sardinia and Turkey defeat Russia?
   a) The Crimean War
   b) The Boer War
   c) The Wars of the Roses

d) The Gulf War

4. Which US President approved the dropping of atom bombs
    on Japan?
    a) Richard Nixon
    b) Harry S. Truman
    c) Dwight D. Eisenhower
    d) Franklin D. Roosevelt

5. With which revolution, occurring in 1789, is the ideology
    'Liberty, equality, fraternity' associated?
    a) The French Revolution
    b) The American Civil War
    c) The Russian Revolution
    d) The Glorious Revolution

6. In World War II, what was the US's M4 General Sherman?
    a) A tank
    b) A breed of dog trained to sniff out bombs
    c) A nuclear bomb
    d) A bulletproof jacket

7. Who gave up armed conquest after the Kalinga War?
    a) Rana Sanga
    b) Maharana Pratap
    c) Ashoka
    d) Samudragupta

8. In which present-day country was the Battle of Waterloo
    fought?
    a) France

b) Germany

c) Belgium

d) Italy

9. Which infamous prison would you associate with the date 14 July 1789?

a) Alcatraz

b) Robben Island

c) The Cellular Jail

d) The Bastille

10. Who was the nawab of Bengal when the Battle of Plassey was fought in 1757?

a) Alivardi Khan

b) Mir Qasim

c) Mir Jafar

d) Siraj-ud-Daulah

11. Which war ended at 11 a.m. on the eleventh day of the eleventh month in 1918?

a) World War I

b) World War II

c) The Crimean War

d) The Gulf War

12. Whom did Daulat Khan, the Governor of Lahore, invite to invade India?

a) Genghis Khan

b) Tamerlane

c) Alexander the Great

d) Babur

13. On 13 May 1940, during World War II, who offered his people only 'blood, toil, tears and sweat' as they struggled to keep their freedom?
a) Dwight D. Eisenhower
b) Sir Winston Churchill
c) Hirohito
d) Neville Chamberlain

14. Which ruler died when British troops stormed Seringapatam in May 1799?
a) Ranjit Singh
b) Shivaji
c) Aurangzeb
d) Tipu Sultan

15. Who defeated King Harold II of England in the Battle of Hastings, fought in 1066?
a) Edward the Confessor
b) Robert the Magnificent
c) William the Conqueror
d) Edgar the Peaceful

16. During World War II, if Il Duce was Benito Mussolini, who was Der Führer?
a) General Franco
b) Adolf Hitler
c) Joseph Stalin
d) Winston Churchill

17. What did Admiral Nelson lose in 1797?
a) His arm

b) His eyesight
c) His voice
d) His leg

18. In which present-day state is the historical site of Haldighati located?
a) Bihar
b) Gujarat
c) Uttar Pradesh
d) Rajasthan

19. With which unfortunate incident would you associate the aircraft Enola Gay?
a) The assassination of Archduke Ferdinand
b) The Hiroshima bombing
c) The attack on Pearl Harbour
d) The disappearance of Subhas Chandra Bose

20. Which historical place connects Ibrahim Lodhi's battle against Babur in 1526, Akbar's victory over Hemu in 1556 and Ahmad Shah Abdali's conflict with the Marathas in 1761?
a) Haldighati
b) Panipat
c) Chausa
d) Buxar

WORDPLAY

1. What word is used to describe a person who has a mania for stealing things?
   a) Hippomaniac
   b) Megalomaniac
   c) Kleptomaniac
   d) Egomaniac

2. If you said *merci beaucoup*, you would have said . . .
   a) 'I am sorry'
   b) 'Thank you very much'
   c) 'Welcome'
   d) 'Good morning'

3. Which of these English words comes from a Hindi word meaning 'rob'?
   a) Cheat
   b) Loot

c) Steal

d) Burgle

4. The term 'astronaut' comes from the Latin words meaning 'space' and . . .
    a) Scientist
    b) Life
    c) Sailor
    d) Knight

5. What does the word 'kremlin' mean in Russian?
    a) Prison
    b) Fortress
    c) School
    d) Church

6. What is the Japanese word for 'tray planted'?
    a) Samurai
    b) Origami
    c) Bonsai
    d) Karate

7. The scientific name of this animal is *Delphinus delphis*. How is this creature better known?
    a) Dhole
    b) Deer
    c) Dingo
    d) Dolphin

8. Which of these words comes from the Norwegian word meaning 'snowshoe'?
   a) Ski
   b) Sledge
   c) Puck
   d) Kayak

9. What would you call an ancient Celtic priest, magician or soothsayer?
   a) Medici
   b) Gladiator
   c) Druid
   d) Samurai

10. What do you call a quiet, gentle song sung to send a child to sleep?
   a) Lullaby
   b) Elegy
   c) Ode
   d) Limerick

11. The word 'reptile' comes from a Latin word meaning . . .
   a) Cold-blooded
   b) Four feet
   c) Slimy
   d) Crawled

12. When are you most likely to wish *'Gung hei fat choi'* to your Chinese friend?
   a) New Year's
   b) Marriage anniversary

c) Birthday
d) First day of work

13. The word 'hygiene' was coined after the Greek goddess of . . .
    a) Beauty
    b) Wealth
    c) Health
    d) Music

14. Which word literally means 'empty orchestra' in Japanese?
    a) Karaoke
    b) Bonsai
    c) Samurai
    d) Kendo

15. A haiku is . . .
    a) A Chinese epic
    b) The Vietnamese word for 'novel'
    c) The first letter of the Thai alphabet
    d) A type of Japanese poem

16. Some cough mixtures have the word 'linctus' in them. What is
    the origin of the term?
    a) 'Contains lime'
    b) 'To be licked'
    c) 'Contains linoleum'
    d) 'Heals tonsilitis'

17. Which word connects El Dorado, Bullion and California?
    a) Star
    b) Apple

c) Gold
d) Pink

18. The word 'poach' means to . . .
    a) Catch animals illegally
    b) Send letters anonymously
    c) Hoard essential items
    d) Tell lies

19. The word 'simian' is used to describe . . .
    a) Sheep
    b) Snakes
    c) Monkeys
    d) Deer

20. The word 'solstice' comes from the Latin phrase meaning . . .
    a) A salt cellar
    b) A five-pointed star
    c) 'The sun has stopped'
    d) 'No sun'

WORLD CUISINE

1. What does the word 'pizza' literally mean in Italian?
  a) Tart
  b) Pie
  c) Biscuit
  d) Custard

2. Which Middle Eastern dish is a deep-fried ball or patty made from ground chickpeas or other pulses?
  a) Baklava
  b) Hummus
  c) Falatel
  d) Baba Ganoush

3. Which of these literally means 'mixed bits' in Chinese?
  a) Chop suey
  b) Chow mein
  c) Mei foon

d) Wonton

4. Spaghetti, macaroni and ravioli are all types of . . .
   a) Paella
   b) Pie
   c) Pizza
   d) Pasta

5. The hamburger is named so because . . .
   a) The chef got the idea while watching *Hamlet*.
   b) It has ham in it.
   c) The chef who created it was nicknamed Ham.
   d) It came from Hamburg in Germany.

6. Just as mutton comes from sheep, venison is the meat of which animal?
   a) Camel
   b) Deer
   c) Yak
   d) Horse

7. If you were eating a wiener, you would be eating a . . .
   a) Frankfurter
   b) Scone
   c) Croissant
   d) Patty

8. Which sauce shares its name with a state in Mexico, with Villahermosa as its capital?
   a) Tabasco
   b) Salsa

c) Ketchup
d) Hummus

9. According to popular legend, which famous person brought the idea of ice cream to Italy?
a) Marco Polo
b) Vasco da Gama
c) James Cook
d) Christopher Columbus

10. What would you generally use with a mortar?
a) Colander
b) Peeler
c) Pestle
d) Spatula

11. The name of which food item means 'twice cooked' in French?
a) Biscuit
b) Pie
c) Pizza
d) Cake

12. If Christmas is associated with cakes, what food item is Good Friday associated with?
a) Custard
b) Bread pudding
c) Hot cross bun
d) Apple pie

13. What is the name of the Japanese dish consisting of small balls or rolls of vinegar-flavoured cold rice served with vegetables, egg or raw seafood?
   a) Tempura
   b) Sashimi
   c) Sushi
   d) Wasabi

14. Which of these is a dish of ice cream with added ingredients such as fruit, nuts and syrup?
   a) Tiramisu
   b) Sundae
   c) Waffle
   d) Cheesecake

15. What is a croissant?
   a) Another name for a hot cross bun
   b) A type of snack made of corn
   c) Another name for marble cake
   d) A crescent-shaped roll

16. What are Cheddar, mozzarella, Edam and Camembert types of?
   a) Spice
   b) Soup
   c) Cheese
   d) Pizza

17. If saffron is often referred to as 'yellow gold', what is known as 'pink gold'?
   a) Crab

b) Beetroot
c) Strawberry
d) Shrimp

18. Traditionally, which world-famous sporting event is associated with strawberries and cream?
   a) Olympic Games
   b) FIFA World Cup
   c) The Championships, Wimbledon
   d) Italian Grand Prix

19. Which character, created by Charles Dickens, is famous for his request, 'Please, sir, I want some more'?
   a) Pip
   b) David Copperfield
   c) Oliver Twist
   d) Samuel Pickwick

20. What is candyfloss?
   a) A sweetened soft drink
   b) A type of kitchen utensil
   c) Spun sugar on a stick
   d) Another name for marzipan

WORLD GEOGRAPHY

1. What is the famous cartographer Gerardus Mercator's contribution to geography?
   a) The Panama Canal
   b) The atlas
   c) The barometer
   d) The wind vane

2. Which desert occupies almost all of Botswana?
   a) Gobi
   b) Sahara
   c) Thar
   d) Kalahari

3. Which country has the most volcanoes of any country in the world?
   a) Sri Lanka
   b) Indonesia

    c) Canada

    d) Japan

4. Which is the only city in the world to straddle two continents—Europe and Asia?
    a) Baku
    b) Istanbul
    c) Kabul
    d) Lisbon

5. Which of these regions is often called the 'lungs of the planet' as it produces about 20 per cent of the world's oxygen?
    a) The Great Barrier Reef
    b) The Amazon rainforest
    c) The Sunderbans
    d) Yellowstone National Park

6. Which of these is a warm wind rushing eastward down the Rocky Mountains of Canada and the USA?
    a) Levant
    b) Sirocco
    c) Loo
    d) Chinook

7. Which waterfall leaps from a flat-topped plateau named Auyán-Tepuí, meaning 'devil's mountain'?
    a) Niagara
    b) Angel
    c) Victoria
    d) Jog

8. Francisco Vázquez de Coronado was the first European to discover which geographical feature?
   a) Stonehenge
   b) The Grand Canyon
   c) Mount Everest
   d) The Sahara desert

9. Which is the southernmost capital city in the world?
   a) La Paz
   b) Canberra
   c) Wellington
   d) Montevideo

10. Which country was formed by the merger of Tanganyika and Zanzibar?
    a) Tanzania
    b) Liberia
    c) Uganda
    d) Kenya

11. A certain group of Australian Aboriginal people call it Uluru and worship it. It is also known as ...
    a) Ayers Rock
    b) Stonehenge
    c) Mount Rushmore
    d) Saser Kangri

12. Which is the only Portuguese-speaking country in South America?
    a) Uruguay
    b) Brazil

c) Chile
d) Paraguay

13. Which river do the three streams Blue, Atbara and White form?
a) Murray
b) Danube
c) Volga
d) Nile

14. Which is the only letter of the English alphabet that does not appear in the name of any US state?
a) V
b) Q
c) X
d) Y

15. Which is the largest country in the world in terms of area?
a) Russia
b) China
c) Canada
d) The USA

16. In 1542, when the Portuguese first sighted this island, they called it Ilha Formosa, meaning 'beautiful island'. By what name is this island now known?
a) Greenland
b) Taiwan
c) Borneo
d) Bali

17. Princess Konohana Sakuya is worshipped as the supernatural deity of which of the following peaks?
a) Kilimanjaro
b) Mount Fuji
c) Aconcagua
d) K2

18. The name of which country comes from the Latin word for 'silver'?
a) Venezuela
b) Argentina
c) Norway
d) Somalia

19. What does the orange colour on the flag of Bhutan signify?
a) Buddhism
b) The king
c) The gemstones found in the country
d) The sun

20. The Galapagos Islands are named after which creature?
a) Elephant
b) Crocodile
c) Tortoise
d) Komodo dragon

WORLD HISTORY

1. What happened at the Boston Tea Party?
   a) Drinking tea was declared illegal.
   b) Three hundred and forty-two chests of tea were dumped into the Boston Harbour by demonstrators.
   c) Tea was served for the first time in the US.
   d) It inspired Lewis Carroll to write *Alice's Adventures in Wonderland*.

2. On which ship did Francis Drake sail around the world?
   a) *Nina*
   b) *Endeavour*
   c) *Santa Maria*
   d) *Golden Hind*

3. After watching a slave woman being sold at an auction, who said, 'By God, boys, if I ever get a chance to hit that thing, I'll hit it and hit it hard'?
   a) Harriet Beecher Stowe
   b) Nelson Mandela
   c) George Washington
   d) Abraham Lincoln

4. *Pravda* was the official newspaper of the Communist Party of the Soviet Union from 1918 to 1991. What does 'pravda' mean in Russian?
   a) Country
   b) Pure
   c) Truth
   d) Revolution

5. In 1933, which word was first used in a pamphlet titled *Now or Never*?
   a) Pakistan
   b) Inquilab
   c) Swaraj
   d) Satyagraha

6. Which Portuguese explorer became a page to Queen Eleanor, wife of John II, in Lisbon at an early age?
   a) Christopher Columbus
   b) Ferdinand Magellan
   c) Marco Polo
   d) Vasco da Gama

7. With which famous personality would you associate the speech 'I Have a Dream'?
   a) Nelson Mandela
   b) Mahatma Gandhi
   c) Martin Luther King Jr
   d) The 14th Dalai Lama

8. Who was the prime minister of the United Kingdom at the time of Queen Elizabeth II's coronation?
   a) Harold Macmillan
   b) Winston Churchill
   c) Clement Attlee
   d) Neville Chamberlain

9. By what name is K'ung-fu-tzu better known to the Western world?
   a) Tavernier
   b) Hiuen Tsang
   c) Confucius
   d) Fa-Hien

10. Who was the last member of the Macedonian Ptolemaic dynasty to rule Egypt?
   a) Alexander
   b) Cleopatra
   c) Nero
   d) Caligula

11. Which ruler's original name was Temüjin?
   a) Genghis Khan
   b) Nero

   c) Nadir Shah

   d) Tamerlane

12. Whose last words were 'Go on, get out. Last words are for fools who haven't said enough'?
   a) Karl Marx
   b) Aristotle
   c) Archimedes
   d) Napoleon

13. According to legend, which instrument was Nero playing while Rome burned?
   a) Drum
   b) Fiddle
   c) Mouth organ
   d) Harp

14. On which famous landmark would you find the words 'Give me your tired, your poor, your huddled masses yearning to breathe free ...'?
   a) The Statue of Liberty
   b) The White House
   c) The Eiffel Tower
   d) Big Ben

15. How many knights sat around King Arthur's Round Table?
   a) 100
   b) 150
   c) 200
   d) 300

16. In 326 BCE, to whom did King Ambhi give troops in return for aid against King Porus?
a) Alexander
b) Napoleon
c) Mahmud of Ghazni
d) Tamerlane

17. In 1524, which famous explorer was buried in St Francis Church, Fort Kochi?
a) Ferdinand Magellan
b) Christopher Columbus
c) Vasco da Gama
d) Amerigo Vespucci

18. Which country was Herodotus referring to when he said, 'There is no country that possesses so many wonders, nor any that has such a number of works which defy description'?
a) Egypt
b) Italy
c) Greece
d) Turkey

19. Besides being US Presidents, what is common to Abraham Lincoln, James Garfield, William McKinley and John F. Kennedy?
a) All four served as vice president first.
b) All four were ambidextrous.
c) All four were assassinated.
d) All four were born on 4 July.

20. Which capital city was formerly called Christiania?
- a) Rome
- b) Paris
- c) Yangon
- d) Oslo

WORLD LITERATURE

1. Edward Lear was famous for his humorous five-line poems. What is the correct term for this kind of poetry?
   a) Limerick
   b) Haiku
   c) Sonnet
   d) Couplet

2. Whose birth name was William Sydney Porter?
   a) George Orwell
   b) Mark Twain
   c) O. Henry
   d) Rudyard Kipling

3. What kind of animal was T.S. Eliot's Macavity?
   a) Bear
   b) Dog

c) Rabbit
d) Cat

4. *Chitty Chitty Bang Bang* is the only children's story by . . .
   a) Agatha Christie
   b) Ian Fleming
   c) Arthur Conan Doyle
   d) Leo Tolstoy

5. 'He was hardly more than five feet four inches but carried himself with great dignity. His head was exactly the shape of an egg, and he always perched it a little on one side.' Who is being described by his assistant in these lines?
   a) Sherlock Holmes
   b) Hercule Poirot
   c) Chacha Chaudhury
   d) Robin Hood

6. Who is the youngest author to receive the Nobel Prize in Literature?
   a) Rudyard Kipling
   b) Ernest Hemingway
   c) Pearl S. Buck
   d) T.S. Eliot

7. Which famous author wrote *Euclid and His Modern Rivals*, a rare example of humorous work concerning mathematics?
   a) Charles Dickens
   b) Mark Twain
   c) Lewis Carroll
   d) Jules Verne

8. In which novel does Jean Valjean steal a loaf of bread and get imprisoned?
   a) *Les Misérables*
   b) *The Count of Monte Cristo*
   c) *Around the World in Eighty Days*
   d) *A Tale of Two Cities*

9. In which Shakespearean play would you read the quote 'To be, or not to be, that is the question'?
   a) *Hamlet*
   b) *Macbeth*
   c) *Othello*
   d) *King Lear*

10. Which of the following is the title of a book about Winston Smith?
   a) *1857*
   b) *1947*
   c) *1984*
   d) *2000*

11. I have a brother named Mycroft. My character is based on the surgeon Dr Joseph Bell. I was created by Sir Arthur Conan Doyle. Who am I?
   a) Sherlock Holmes
   b) Father Brown
   c) Hercule Poirot
   d) C. Auguste Dupin

12. Which author's work, 'How Much Land Does a Man Need?', was called 'the greatest story that the literature of the world knows' by James Joyce?
   a) William Shakespeare
   b) Leo Tolstoy
   c) Albert Camus
   d) Victor Hugo

13. Yahoo is the name of an uncouth tribe in which well-known book?
   a) *A Journey to the Centre of the Earth*
   b) *Robinson Crusoe*
   c) *Gulliver's Travels*
   d) *Adventures of Huckleberry Finn*

14. Which famous English author was born in 1903 in Motihari, Bihar?
   a) George Orwell
   b) Rudyard Kipling
   c) Ruskin Bond
   d) Roald Dahl

15. What was W.B. Yeats referring to when he said, 'I have carried the manuscripts of these translations around with me for days, reading it in trains or on the top of buses and in restaurants. I have often had to close it lest some stranger should see how much it moved me'?
   a) *Gitanjali*
   b) *A Passage to India*

c) 1984
d) *The Great Gatsby*

16. Which Nobel Prize–winning author wrote *A House for Mr Biswas*?
    a) William Butler Yeats
    b) Rabindranath Tagore
    c) Rudyard Kipling
    d) V.S. Naipaul

17. Which author was known by the pseudonym Saki?
    a) H.H. Munro
    b) Guy de Maupassant
    c) Oscar Wilde
    d) O. Henry

18. In William Shakespeare's *The Merchant of Venice*, from whose body does Shylock wish to take a pound of flesh?
    a) Solanio
    b) Bassanio
    c) Lysander
    d) Antonio

19. With which fictional character is the colour Lincoln green associated?
    a) Zorro
    b) Jack Sparrow
    c) Robin Hood
    d) Don Juan

20. Which George Bernard Shaw play begins with 'Covent Garden at 11.15 p.m. Torrents of heavy summer rain'?
a) Candida
b) Man and Superman
c) Arms and the Man
d) Pygmalion

THE BQC JINGLE

AN ARTICLE BY SHANKAR–EHSAAN–LOY

When Shankar–Ehsaan–Loy composed the unforgettable jingle for the Bournvita Quiz Contest so many years ago, they were not the household name they are today. In this short essay, they fondly reminisce about creating the music for the catchy jingle.

> 'Duniya mein jitney jawaab, unse hain zyada sawaal,
> Sawaalon se dosti kar lo, inhi se hotey hain kamaal,
> If we know it, at the right time,
> If we know it, at the right time,
> Kya kehna, we're the best,
> We're winners, coz we made it,
> To the Bournvita Quiz Contest!'

Our association with the *Bournvita Quiz Contest*, the iconic show, was really memorable. The show was an integral part of our youth and schooldays. We had grown up listening to Ameen Sayani hosting BQC on radio. We would follow the show right till the end as we were interested in trivia and general knowledge. Very often we didn't get the answers right, but it was amazing to see schoolkids with so much knowledge. It was fun!

When we first met Tess Joseph, who went on to become co-director of the show, she was collaborating with Leslie Lewis for BQC and we were doing the background score of *Dil Chahta Hai*. We were not very well known back then and were still looking for our big break. One or two years later, Tess approached us and asked us to create a new title track for the *Bournvita Quiz Contest*. We readily agreed. It was our pleasure to be a part of the legendary show that had been such a big part of our childhood.

The lyrics were not written by us. We remember they were sent to us by Derek's team. All we did was compose the music. The process was very simple, and it really didn't take us very long to do it. We went on Google and searched around for some inspiration. The lyrics were catchy; and after experimenting a bit, we knew we had a 'winner' of a tune. We recorded throughout the day and were quite satisfied with the end result. A few months later, we were invited on the show as well. By that time, *Dil Chahta Hai* had just released. We even remember singing on the show.

Who was to know that the BQC jingle would become so popular? It's been some time since we last heard the song. We would love to hear it again. We are sure it will bring back many nostalgic memories. The *Bournvita Quiz Contest* jingle was one of our first hits and holds a very special place in our hearts.

WORLD MYTHS

1. What special attribute did the mythical bird phoenix have?
   a) It could rise from its ashes after burning itself.
   b) It could read the minds of others.
   c) It could turn others to gold.
   d) It could be in hell and heaven at the same time

2. What was the first of Hercules's Twelve Labours?
   a) Killing the Nemean lion
   b) Capturing the wild boar of Mount Erymanthus
   c) Capturing the elusive female red deer of Arcadia
   d) Killing the Lernaean Hydra

3. In Roman mythology, how is Cupid depicted?
   a) An old man with a staff
   b) A winged infant with a bow and arrows
   c) A middle-aged man with a chalice in his hand
   d) A lean man with a hammer

4. Which bird gets its name from a mythical watchman with a hundred eyes?
a) Nyctimene
b) Argus
c) Peacock
d) Phoenix

5. Which Greek goddess shares her name with a part of the human body?
a) Leto
b) Iris
c) Rhea
d) Hebe

6. In Norse mythology, Mjöllnir is the hammer of which god?
a) Odin
b) Thor
c) Loki
d) Tyr

7. Ra was the Egyptian god of the . . .
a) Sun
b) Dead
c) Underworld
d) Sea

8. Which mischievous Greek god had the horns, legs and ears of a goat?
a) Pan
b) Ares

c) Hephaestus

d) Thanatos

9. Which planet is named after the Roman god of war?
    a) Mars
    b) Neptune
    c) Jupiter
    d) Mercury

10. According to the Greek poet Homer, heaven was located on the summit of which mountain?
    a) Etna
    b) Olympus
    c) Vesuvius
    d) Parnassus

11. The head of the Egyptian deity Anubis resembled the head of which animal?
    a) Fox
    b) Hyena
    c) Wolf
    d) Jackal

12. In Greek mythology, who opened a box and released all evils into the world?
    a) Demeter
    b) Pandora
    c) Achlys
    d) Hemera

13. Zeus was the father of the Greek muses. Who was their mother?
 a) Mnemosyne
 b) Hera
 c) Artemis
 d) Hestia

14. Which legendary British king was the son of King Uther Pendragon?
 a) King Arthur
 b) Constantine the Great
 c) Ambrosius Aurelianus
 d) King Aldroenus

15. The Greek nymph Echo's hopeless love for Narcissus made her fade away until only . . .
 a) Her ashes remained
 b) Her voice remained
 c) Her footsteps remained
 d) Her magic wand remained

16. In Norse mythology, who was sent by Odin to the battlefields to choose the slain?
 a) Cyclops
 b) Sphinx
 c) Valkyrie
 d) Dionysus

17. Which mythical ruler had the 'golden touch'?
 a) Asmodeus
 b) Midas

c) Amlawdd Wledig
d) Gard Agdi

18. Which country did Moses lead his people out of?
    a) Egypt
    b) Israel
    c) Syria
    d) Libya

19. Which part of Achilles's body was his weakest point?
    a) His ankle
    b) His heel
    c) His wrist
    d) His neck

20. Name the most famous gorgon that had snakes for hair.
    a) Andromeda
    b) Medusa
    c) Athena
    d) Aphrodite

WORLD TOUR

1. Which of these monuments is located in Piazza dei Miracoli, or the Square of Miracles?
   a) The sphinx
   b) The Eiffel Tower
   c) The Sydney Opera House
   d) The Leaning Tower of Pisa

2. The population of which country consists mostly of Flemings and Walloons?
   a) Finland
   b) Sweden
   c) Austria
   d) Belgium

3. What is the colour of the Golden Gate Bridge in San Francisco?
   a) Antique gold

b) Cherry red
c) International orange
d) Indigo blue

4. The Great Barrier Reef is the largest collection of coral reefs in the world. It is located off the north-east coast of . . .
   a) Australia
   b) Indonesia
   c) Japan
   d) Iceland

5. In June 1885, what was brought to New York Harbor in a French ship called *Isere*?
   a) The Statue of Liberty
   b) The Leaning Tower of Pisa
   c) The Lincoln Memorial
   d) The White House

6. A statue of which fictional character in Copenhagen is a popular tourist attraction?
   a) Rapunzel
   b) Little Mermaid
   c) Cinderella
   d) Snow White

7. Which one of the seven wonders of the ancient world can still be seen today?
   a) The pyramids of Giza
   b) The Hanging Gardens of Babylon
   c) The Pharos of Alexandria
   d) The Colossus of Rhodes

8. If you were on the summit of the tallest free-standing mountain in the world, you would be on Mount...
a) Fuji
b) Kilimanjaro
c) Kanchenjunga
d) Aconcagua

9. Which city would you be in if you passed under the Bridge of Sighs?
a) Prague
b) Venice
c) San Francisco
d) Dublin

10. The Bronx, Brooklyn, Queens, Staten Island and Manhattan together form which city?
a) New York City
b) Boston
c) Houston
d) San Francisco

11. After which famous person is the airport in Liverpool named?
a) John Lennon
b) Agatha Christie
c) William Shakespeare
d) Jane Austen

12. In which capital city would you find the Temple of the Emerald Buddha?
a) Bangkok
b) Colombo

c) Taipei

d) Beijing

13. With which city would you associate Checkpoint Charlie?

a) Moscow

b) Paris

c) London

d) Berlin

14. If you were visiting the Archaeological Areas of Pompeii, Herculaneum and Torre Annunziata, which country would you be in?

a) Italy

b) Germany

c) France

d) Spain

15. What is located just east of the Palatine Hill, on the grounds of what was Nero's Golden House?

a) The Colosseum

b) The sphinx

c) Uluru

d) Stonehenge

16. If you were visiting Myanmar, which currency would you need?

a) Baht

b) Riyal

c) Kyat

d) Dinar

17. Which famous monument is affectionately called the Coat Hanger?
a) The Sydney Harbour Bridge
b) The Eiffel Tower
c) The Empire State Building
d) Big Ben

18. Which monument was built for the International Exposition of 1889 to celebrate the centenary of the French Revolution?
a) The Statue of Liberty
b) The Leaning Tower of Pisa
c) The Eiffel Tower
d) Qutub Minar

19. Which landmark is located on 1600 Pennsylvania Avenue, NW, Washington, DC, 20500?
a) The White House
b) The Statue of Liberty
c) Disneyland
d) Times Square

20. Name the tourist attraction that lies on the border between Ontario, Canada, and New York State, the US.
a) The Golden Gate Bridge
b) Niagara Falls
c) Mount Rushmore
d) Yellowstone National Park

GUESTS OF HONOUR

A LIST OF CELEBRITIES WHO HAVE APPEARED ON THE SHOW

In the early years of BQC, there was a special round on the show wherein a celebrity guest was invited to ask questions of the participants. Here is a list of those distinguished 'quizmasters' who appeared on the iconic quiz.

Aamir Khan	Amit Kumar
Abey Kuruvilla	Amjad Ali Khan
Aditi Govitrikar	Anaida
Adnan Sami	Anita Pratap
Ajay Jadeja	Anjali Bhagwat
Ajit Pal Singh	Annu Kapoor
Ajit Wadekar	Anu Malik
Alka Yagnik	Anup Jalota
Alyque Padamsee	Anupam Kher
Ameen Sayani	Anuradha Paudwal

Arjun Rampal
Aryan Vaid
Asha Bhosle
Asha Parekh
Ashish Vidyarthi
Ashwini Nachappa
Atul Kasbekar
Babul Supriyo
Bhaichung Bhutia
Bhupen Hazarika
Bipasha Basu
Bishan Singh Bedi
Celina Jaitly
Chandrachur Singh
Cyrus Broacha
Dalip Tahil
Debashree Roy
Devang Patel
Diana Edulji
Diana Hayden
Dibyendu Barua
Divya Seth
Eknath Solkar
Farooq Shaikh
Gary Lawyer
Hariharan
Hariprasad Chaurasia
Harsha Bhogle
Hema Malini
Ila Arun
Inder Kumar Gujral

Indus Creed
Jagmohan Dalmiya
Jaidip Mukerjea
Javagal Srinath
Javed Akhtar
Javed Jaffrey
Jaya Bachchan
Jug Suraiya
Juhi Chawla
Julio Francis Ribeiro
Kabir Bedi
Kalpana Lajmi
Kanwaljit Singh
Kavita Krishnamurthy
Khushwant Singh
Kiran Bedi
Kiran Uttam Ghosh
Kirron Kher
Kumar Sanu
L. Subramaniam
Leslie Lewis
Lillete Dubey
Louis Banks
Lucky Ali
Luke Kenny
Lymaraina D'Souza
Mahesh Bhatt
Mahima Chaudhary
Malaika Arora
Mani Shankar Aiyar
Manish Malhotra

Maria Goretti | Renuka Shahane
Merwyn Fernandes | Robin Singh
Michael Ferreira | Roger Binny
Milind Soman | Rohini Hattangadi
Monideepa Banerjee | Rohit Bal
Mukesh Khanna | Roopa Ganguly
Munish Makhija | Roshan Abbas
Nafisa Ali | Ruby Bhatia
Nafisa Joseph | S. Venkataraghavan
Nandita Das | Saba Karim
Neil O'Brien | Sabyasachi Mukherjee
Noyonika Chatterjee | Sachin Khedekar
Omung Kumar | Sagarika
P. Gopichand | Sanjana Kapoor
P.K. Banerjee | Sanjay Dutt
Pallavi Joshi | Sanjay Manjrekar
Pandit Jasraj | Sanjeev Kapoor
Pankaj Udhas | Shaan
Prabhudeva | Shabana Azmi
Prakash Padukone | Shankar Mahadevan
Preeti Sagar | Sharbari Dutta
Pritish Nandy | Sharmila Tagore
Priya Tendulkar | Shatrughan Sinha
R. Madhavan | Shekhar Suman
Raageshwari | Shenaz Treasurywala
Rahul Bose | Shivkumar Sharma
Rakshanda Khan | Shobhaa De
Ramakant Achrekar | Shyam Benegal
Raveena Tandon | Sivamani
Ravi Shastri | Sonu Nigam
Reema Lagoo | Soumitra Roy

Sudha Chandran Usha Uthup
Suneeta Rao V.V.S. Laxman
Suniel Shetty Vani Ganapathy
Sunil Dutt Venkatesh Prasad
Suresh Oberoi Vijay Tendulkar
Swaroop Sampat Vinod Dua
Syed Kirmani Vir Sanghvi
T.N. Seshan Wilson Jones
Talat Aziz Yukta Mookhey
Tanuja Yuvraj Singh
Tanuja Chandra Zafar Iqbal
Tanusree Shankar Zakir Hussain
Upamanyu Chatterjee Zeenat Aman

ANSWERS

1. To tell other bees where to find food
2. Lions
    A pride usually has several generations of lionesses, a few breeding males and their cubs. The average number of members in a pride is fifteen.
3. Hippopotamus
    This fluid acts as a skin moisturizer, water repellent and antibiotic. It appears red when exposed to direct sunlight.
4. Butterflies
5. Elephant
6. The only floating national park in the world
    The park is located in the south-western part of Loktak Lake.
7. King cobra
    It uses dead leaves, soil and ground litter to make its nest.
8. Spider
    It has an hourglass-shaped design on its abdomen.
9. Cheetah
10. Brush
11. W-shaped pupils
12. Orangutan
13. Pekingese
    The breed was developed in ancient China. It was introduced to the West by English forces that looted the Imperial Palace in Peking (now Beijing) in 1860.
14. Lay eggs
    It is a member of the egg-laying mammalian order Monotremata.
15. Mauritius

16. Carry the eggs and give birth to young ones
    The female seahorse places her eggs in a brood pouch located at the base of the male's tail, where the eggs are later fertilized.
17. Octopus
18. A stag
19. Liger
20. Silverfish

ART AND CULTURE

1. Michelangelo
2. Rabindranath Tagore
   He invited Atomba Singh to teach at his school in Santiniketan.
3. *The Thinker*
   It is called *Le Penseur* in French.
4. Walls
5. M.F. Husain
6. Ganesha
7. Wax
8. His face would be painted green.
9. Rukmini Devi Arundale
   It was founded in Chennai in 1936.
10. A district in Bihar
    It is also referred to as Mithila art. It has traditionally been done by the women of the area.
11. Folding paper to make interesting things
12. Odissi
    It is the dance form of Odisha.
13. Jesus Christ with his disciples

14. Blue pottery
    Some of the most common objects created using this art form
    are ashtrays, tiles, flower pots, lampshades, jars, accessories, etc.
15. Karnataka
    Bidriware includes metal objects decorated with a type of
    Indian inlay work.
16. Krishna
17. Zardozi
18. Kathak
19. Tanjore painting
    Tanjore paintings generally depict Hindu gods and goddesses
    and the legends surrounding them.
20. Graffiti

ASTRONOMY

1. The three Apollo 11 astronauts—Armstrong, Aldrin and Collins
2. Galileo Galilei
   He first observed these satellites in 1610, and that is why they
   are also called the Galilean moons.
3. Dog
   Laika travelled aboard Sputnik 2, launched on 3 November
   1957 by the Soviet Union. This mission was meant to test the
   safety of space travel for human beings.
4. The sun
5. Nicolaus Copernicus
6. None
7. Long-haired
8. The largest volcano on Mars and also in the solar system
   A shield volcano, Olympus Mons has a diameter of 624
   kilometres and a height of 25 kilometres. It is rimmed by a
   6-kilometre-high scarp.

9. Neptune
10. The appearance of Halley's Comet
   Mark Twain was born in 1835, the same year that Halley's Comet made an appearance. He died in the year of its next appearance, 1910.
11. Saturn
12. Jantar Mantar, Jaipur
   It was built by Sawai Jai Singh in 1734.
13. *'Saare jahaan se achcha.'*
14. Characters from the works of Alexander Pope and Shakespeare
   Juliet, Puck, Cordelia, Ophelia, Bianca, Desdemona, Portia, Rosalind, Cressida and Belinda are some of the moons of the planet.
15. Libra
16. Dog Star
17. Aryabhata
   It was launched by a Soviet Kosmos-3M rocket from Kapustin Yar on 19 April 1975.
18. Separate galaxy beyond the Milky Way
19. Kalpana Chawla
20. Mercury

AWARDS

1. Mahatma Gandhi
2. A peepul leaf
   The Bharat Ratna is the highest civilian honour in India. It is awarded for exceptional service towards advancements in art, literature and science, as well as in recognition of public service of the highest order.

3. Best editing
4. He was the first cricketer to be knighted while still playing the game.
5. Hindi and English
6. C.V. Raman
7. Devika Rani
The Dadasaheb Phalke Award is given to a person associated with the film industry, for their outstanding contribution to the growth and development of Indian cinema.
8. Youngest person to win the prize
She won the award for her second novel, *The Inheritance of Loss*.
9. Jnanpith Award
Vagdevi is another name for Saraswati, the goddess of learning.
10. Children's literature
11. J.R.D. Tata
12. It comprised one big Oscar statuette and seven little ones.
13. The Philippines
The award is presented to the winners at formal ceremonies held in Manila, Philippines, on 31 August every year.
14. The Palme d'Or
15. Mother Teresa
Mother Teresa was born Agnes Gonxha Bojaxhiu in Skopje, Macedonia, in 1910. Her family was of Albanian descent.
16. John F. Kennedy
17. Rabindranath Tagore
He received it in 1913.
18. The World Scout Committee
19. The Ashok Chakra

20. C.V. Raman

He received the Nobel Prize in 1930 and the Bharat Ratna in 1954.

CARTOONS AND COMICS

1. Sabu

The fifteen-foot-tall alien is from Jupiter.

2. Jellystone National Park

3. Obelix

4. Snoopy

He is a dog from the comic strip *Peanuts*, created by Charles Schulz.

5. They are his nephews.

6. Superman

He was raised as Clark Kent.

7. Noddy

He lives in Toyland.

8. Irona

9. Bruce Wayne

He is also known as Batman.

10. Dog

11. Spiderman

His real name is Peter Benjamin Parker.

12. R.K. Laxman

13. Mandrake

Mandrake the Magician is a comic strip created by Lee Falk and Phil Davis.

14. Popeye

15. Mickey Mouse

16. Superman
    He was born on the doomed planet Krypton.
17. The Phantom
18. Spider
19. Archie
20. Postman
    He is the most common target of Dennis's mischief.

CHEMISTRY

1. Platinum
2. It is used as a stenching agent to detect leaks.
3. Robert Bunsen
4. Radium
5. Chlorine
6. Diamond
   The extreme hardness of the gemstone makes it a good choice for a number of important industrial uses.
7. The Latin word for 'rainbow'
8. Aspirin
9. Gas
10. Copper
11. Inert gases
    They are also known as noble gases. They make up group 18 (VIIIA) of the periodic table.
12. Vinegar
13. Carbon
    It makes up about 0.025 per cent of the earth's crust.
14. Calcium oxide
15. Tin
16. Methane

17. Carbon paper
18. Water
It can dissolve more substances than any other liquid.
19. Nitrogen
20. Polonium

CHILDREN'S FILMS

1. *101 Dalmatians*
2. *Aladdin*
Robin Williams lent his voice to the Genie.
3. Meerkat
In Swahili, the name Simba means 'lion'.
4. Julie Andrews
It fetched her an Oscar for Best Actress in a Leading Role, her first.
5. Saber-toothed tiger
6. *Koi Mil Gaya*
In the film, Rohit Mehra is given special powers by a blue-skinned alien named Jadoo.
7. *Garfield*
The film is inspired by a comic strip created by Jim Davis.
8. A dolphin
9. *My Dear Kuttichathan*
It was later dubbed in Hindi as *Chhota Chetan*.
10. Wildcats
11. Hugo
The film is based on a novel by Victor Hugo.
12. *Pocahontas*
13. A tiffin box
In 2012, Partho A. Gupte, who played the protagonist, Stanley, won the National Film Award for Best Child Artist.

14. Jurassic Park

It was conceptualized in a novel of the same name by Michael Crichton, which was later developed into a film franchise.

15. *Toy Story*

16. Laurel and Hardy

17. *The Sound of Music*

The film is based on Maria von Trapp's 1949 memoir, *The Story of the Trapp Family Singers*.

18. The Great Barrier Reef

19. A hen

20. Ruskin Bond

CHILDREN'S LITERATURE

1. Cinderella

Her stepmother's name is Lady Tremaine.

2. Peter Pan

The character first appeared in James Barrie's 1902 novel *The Little White Bird*.

3. *Robinson Crusoe*

The novel was written by Daniel Defoe and published in 1719.

4. Hans Christian Andersen

The Danish writer is famous for works such as 'The Little Mermaid', 'The Ugly Duckling' and 'Thumbelina'.

5. 'If'

6. The Count of Monte Cristo

The novel, of the same name, was published in French as *Le Comte de Monte-Cristo* in 1844–45.

7. *The Last of the Mohicans*

8. *Uncle Tom's Cabin*

9. *Moby Dick*

10. *The Hundred and One Dalmatians*
11. *Treasure Island*
    The story is set in the mid-1700s, first along the coast of western England and then in the seaport of Bristol.
12. *Nautilus*
    Published in 1870, *Twenty Thousand Leagues under the Sea* is a classic science fiction novel by Jules Verne.
13. His father
14. *The Hunchback of Notre Dame*
    The novel powerfully evokes medieval life in the city of Paris during the reign of Louis XI.
15. *Alice's Adventures in Wonderland*
    Only twenty-two known copies of the original exist since Lewis Carroll withdrew the entire print run.
16. The name of the cow that Jack traded for some beans
17. Raksha
18. J.K. Rowling
19. Sheep
20. Thumbelina

CLOTHES AND ACCESSORIES

1. Kimono
   Worn by Japanese men and women, it is an ankle-length gown with long, expansive sleeves and a V-neck.
2. His glove
3. Arunachal Pradesh
4. Duffel bag
5. Khaki
   It is a light-brown fabric used primarily for military uniforms. It is made of cotton, wool or combinations of these fibres, as well

as with blends of synthetic fibres. It is available in a variety of weaves, such as serge.

6. Patola
7. Chikankari
8. Tattooing
9. They prevented the pockets from tearing under the weight of tools and increased their durability.
10. Hands
11. Kerala
    The word 'calico' comes from Calicut, now known as Kozhikode.
12. Hats
    The word 'sombrero' comes from the Spanish word *sombra*, meaning 'shade'.
13. Achkan
14. Shoes
    The device was invented by Charles F. Brannock and patented in 1926.
15. Head
    It is a skullcap that is traditionally worn by male Orthodox Jews.
16. Bhutan
    It is a knee-length robe that is tied at the waist by a traditional belt known as *kera*.
17. Perukes, or men's wig
18. Knees
19. Iraq
20. Silk

COMPUTERS AND THE INTERNET

1. Computer mouse

2. Zero and one
3. Java
   The language Java was created at Sun Microsystems, Inc.
4. Sending the first email
   Tomlinson sent the first email from one computer to another, both in the same room, so that he could check if the software worked.
5. It is half a byte.
   A byte is a group of binary digits or bits (usually eight in total), operated on as a unit.
6. Trojan horse
7. Virtual community
8. Esc
9. Charles Babbage
10. Spain
11. World Wide Web
12. Fonts
13. The human brain
14. Alternate
15. Read-Only Memory
    It is the memory that is read at high speed but is not capable of being changed by programme instructions.
16. Element
    A pixel is a minute area of illumination on a display screen, one of many that make up an image.
17. Keyboard
18. Many
19. Mouse
    It is a small ball that is set in a holder and can be rotated by hand to move a cursor on a computer screen.
20. Lord Byron

1. 9994
   Bradman's Test batting average was 99.94.
2. It was introduced by players from Yorkshire.
3. Black Caps
4. Sachin Tendulkar
   In 1992, on the second day of the Durban Test series, Tendulkar was caught short of the crease. He was dismissed on the basis of TV replays. Karl Liebenberg of South Africa was the third umpire in the match.
5. Eden Gardens
   It was designed in 1841, when Lord Auckland was the British governor general of India.
6. West Indies
   The match was played on 31 October 1976 at the M. Chinnaswamy Stadium, Bangalore (now Bengaluru).
7. Pre-Independence tournament
8. W.G. Grace
9. Ashes
10. Yuvraj Singh
    His father is Yograj Singh.
11. A helmet
12. Asia
13. Sunil Gavaskar
    He scored 188 in the first innings and a duck in the second.
14. At the boundary, directly behind the wicketkeeper
15. Timed out
16. K.S. Ranjitsinhji
17. Be a runner
    He was a runner for Parthiv Patel during the fourth ODI between India and England at Lord's in September 2011.

18. Him being a champion marble player as a child
19. Change of decision
20. Scuffing

DISEASES AND DISORDERS

1. He was given the first vaccination against smallpox by Edward Jenner.
2. Brain
3. Hair loss
4. Thyroid gland
   The thyroid secretes hormones that are important for metabolism and growth.
5. Chickenpox
6. Teeth
7. Red and green
8. Jaundice
   It causes a yellow, and sometimes even greenish, discoloration of the skin.
9. Liver
10. Iron deficiency
11. Kidney
    Ronald Lee Herrick donated a kidney to his identical twin, Richard, in an operation performed on 23 December 1954.
12. Lungs
    Infection, inhalation of foreign particles or irradiation are some of the causes of pneumonia.
13. The bite of female anopheles mosquitoes
14. Dandruff
15. Vitamin C
16. Clove oil

17. Bad breath
Halitosis is the technical term for bad breath.
18. Diabetes
19. Smallpox
It is an acute infectious disease that begins with a high fever and back pain, leading to skin eruptions. It was also one of the first diseases to be controlled by a vaccine.
20. Migraine
It is characterized by painful recurring headaches, often accompanied by nausea and vomiting.

FAMOUS WOMEN

1. Agatha Christie
Her works have sold more than 100 million copies and have been translated into nearly 100 languages.
2. Helen Keller
Sullivan remained with Keller from 1887 until her own death in October 1936.
3. Queen Victoria
She lent her name to an era—the Victorian age.
4. Marie Curie
She, along with Henri Becquerel and Pierre Curie, received the Nobel Prize in Physics in 1903.
5. M.S. Subbulakshmi
6. Become prime minister of a country
She became the prime minister of Sri Lanka in 1960.
7. Valentina Tereshkova
She was launched into space aboard Vostok 6 on 16 June 1963.
8. Ada Lovelace
The early programming language Ada was named in her honour.

9. Chimpanzees
10. Margaret Thatcher
11. Mother Teresa
    Nirmal Hriday means 'place for the pure of heart'.
12. Kiran Bedi
13. Amelia Earhart
    She was the first woman to fly alone over the Atlantic Ocean.
14. Annie Besant
15. *Nursing*
16. Vijaya Lakshmi Pandit
    She had a long diplomatic career. She also led the Indian delegation to the United Nations (1946–48, 1952–53).
17. Mars
18. Aung San Suu Kyi
19. Benazir Bhutto
    She was the first woman leader of a Muslim nation in modern history.
20. The Hundred Years' War
    Joan of Arc led the French army to a momentous victory in Orléans. She is also known as the Maid of Orléans.

FICTION

1. A dispute over whether to break the broad or narrow end of an egg
   Gulliver's Travels is a four-part satirical novel by Jonathan Swift.
2. *A Christmas Carol*
   In the October of 1843, Charles Dickens began work on this book to help supplement his family's income.
3. Hedwig
   The highly intelligent owl is a gift from Hagrid.

4. Anna Sewell
   The thought of writing such a piece occurred to her after reading an essay on animals by Horace Bushnell.
5. Twenty years
   This happens to Rip Van Winkle after he accepts a drink of liquor from a group of dwarfs playing ninepins.
6. Nancy Drew
   The Nancy Drew series was published between 1930 and 2003. Some people consider the first fifty-six instalments of this series to be the original series.
7. *Malgudi*
   Malgudi Days is a collection of thirty-two fictional stories set in this beautiful little town.
8. Bear
9. He is trapped in a cave and dies of starvation.
10. Kitty
11. Peter Pan
12. *Animal Farm*
    This book is a political fable based on the events of Russia's Bolshevik revolution and the betrayal of the cause by Joseph Stalin.
13. Robin Hood
    This outlaw appears in a series of stories, some of which date back to as early as the fourteenth century.
14. Goldilocks
15. Scamper
16. *Moby Dick*
17. The Queen of Hearts
18. Sat in the chimney corner, among cinders, after work
19. *Arabian Nights*
20. Brown bear

1. Lala Lajpat Rai
   He was leading a procession to demonstrate against the Simon Commission when he was injured badly.
2. Indira Gandhi
   She also founded the Bal Charkha Sangh in her childhood.
3. Uttar Pradesh
   The robbery took place in Kakori, about 16 kilometres north-west of Lucknow.
4. Lokmanya Tilak
5. He misrepresented his age.
6. Mahatma Gandhi
   The line was written about his departure from South Africa.
7. *'Jai Hind'*
8. C. Rajagopalachari
   He led 100 chosen Congress volunteers across more than 200 kilometres.
9. Quit India Movement
   On 8 August 1942, a meeting of the All India Congress Committee (AICC) was organized in Bombay with the agenda of launching a movement urging the British government to leave India.
10. Abdul Ghaffar Khan
    He was the foremost twentieth-century leader of the Pashtuns, or Pathans.
11. Mangal Pandey
    The film, of the same name, revolves around the Sepoy Mutiny of 1857.
12. Bal Gangadhar Tilak
13. Jawaharlal Nehru

14. Subhas Chandra Bose
15. Satyagraha
16. Dadabhai Naoroji
17. George Yule
18. Revolution
19. The Chauri Chaura incident
    On 4 February 1922, supporters of the Khilafat Movement and the Indian National Congress clashed with local police.
20. On the birth of Indira Gandhi

GEOGRAPHICAL TERMS

1. From the practice of throwing horses overboard from becalmed ships to save water
2. Sand dunes
3. Hurricanes
   From 1954 to 1978, hurricanes were named solely after women.
4. Moraine
5. Isohyet
6. Harmattan
7. Delta
   The geographical feature is named after the shape of the Greek letter.
8. Isthmus
9. 'Opposite to the Arctic'
10. Tundra
11. Igneous
    Granite and gabbro are examples of this type of rock.
12. Topography

13. Eye
14. Rock
15. Tornado
16. Curls of hair
17. Acid rain
18. Barometer
    There are two main types of barometers: mercury and aneroid.
19. Crater
20. Stalagmite

GEOGRAPHY OF INDIA

1. Darjeeling
2. Waterfalls
3. Only active volcano
4. Arunachal Pradesh
   It became an Indian state in 1987.
5. Majuli
6. They were barred from buying land.
7. Gujarat
   The coastline stretches for approximately 1214.70 kilometres.
8. Patna
9. Nagpur
   The marker site was identified in the Great Trigonometrical Survey of India.
10. Narmada
11. Lakshadweep
12. The Ajanta Caves
    These caves are located in Aurangabad, Maharashtra.
13. A trumpet

14. Mumbai

However, Charles II did not want the trouble of ruling these islands and, in 1668, persuaded the East India Company to rent them for just £10 of gold a year.

15. June

16. Mahanadi

17. Gujarat

18. Digboi

It is located in Assam.

19. Kerala

20. Lonar

It is located in Maharashtra, named after the demon Lonasura and ringed by fascinating temples.

HINDI FILMS

1. Amitabh Bachchan

He had a triple role in the film, which was a remake of the blockbuster Kannada film *Shankar Guru*.

2. Rajinikanth

He made his debut in *Katha Sangama* (1975) and became a star with *Apoorva Raagangal* (1975).

3. *Mother India*

It was nominated for an Oscar in 1958. The film was directed by Mehboob Khan and had Nargis in the lead role.

4. Akshay Kumar

5. Yash Chopra

6. Dilip Kumar

He won the award for *Azaad* (1955), *Devdas* (1956) and *Naya Daur* (1957) respectively.

7. Hrithik Roshan

8. Munshi Premchand
   It was Satyajit Ray's first Hindi film.
9. Sanjay Leela Bhansali
10. Aishwarya Rai
11. Sharmila Tagore
    She played the female lead in many Hindi films, including
    Kashmir ki Kali and *An Evening in Paris*.
12. Amitabh Bachchan
13. Karan Johar
14. Ashoka
15. Danny Denzongpa
    The film was released on 15 August 1975.
16. Topi
    The song was sung by Mukesh.
17. Vidya Balan
    She played the role of Radhika Mathur in *Hum Paanch*.
18. Satyajit Ray
19. Arundhati Roy
    The role of Francis Massey was played by Raghuvir Yadav.
20. *Agneepath*

HUMAN BODY

1. Teeth
   It is known as the dental formula.
2. Eyes
3. Ribs
4. Skin
   Its thickness can vary from 0.5 millimetre on the eyelids to
   4 millimetres or more on the palms of the hands and the soles
   of the feet.

5. Nosebleed
6. Blood pressure
7. Fractures
8. Femur
   It is also called the thigh bone.
9. Lung
10. Hiccup
11. Iron
12. Lungs
13. Armpits
14. You would not be able to speak.
    The larynx is also called the voice box.
15. Heart
16. O
17. Stomach
18. Calcium
19. X-rays
20. Ear

INDIA

1. Red Fort
   The Indian republic and its constitution came into force on 26 January 1950, celebrated annually as Republic Day.
2. A lantern
3. Rabindranath Tagore
4. The Indian national flag
5. The raja of Puri
   This ritual is known as *chhera pahanra*.
6. Urdu
   Contemporary banknotes have fifteen languages on the panel, which appears on the reverse of the note.

7. *'Saare Jahaan Se Achcha'*
   This song was originally a poem that was published in the weekly journal *Ittehad* on 16 August 1904.
8. Mother Teresa
9. Coconut palm
10. Karnataka
    Traditionally Hampi was known as Pampakshetra of Kishkindha. It is situated on the southern bank of the Tungabhadra River. Once it was the seat of the Vijayanagara Empire.
11. Red Fort
12. Speak Sanskrit on a regular basis
13. Haryana
14. The ninth Asian Games
15. Bihu
    It is the most important festival in Assam.
16. Pongal
17. Rats
18. Kerala
19. Jawaharlal Nehru
    He was cremated here after his death on 27 May 1964.
20. *'Jana Gana Mana'*

INDIAN CUISINE

1. Nargisi kofta
2. Kulcha
   A kulcha is a small, round Indian bread made from flour, milk and butter, typically stuffed with meat or vegetables.
3. Bhujia
4. Parsi

5. Goa
6. Sweet
   The essential ingredients of Mysore pak are ghee, chickpea flour and sugar.
7. Milk
   Operation Flood was launched in 1970.
8. Tamarind
9. Asaf-ud-Daulah
   In 1784, during a famine in Awadh, Nawab Asaf-ud-Daulah initiated a food-for-work programme, employing thousands in the construction of the Bada Imambara. Large cauldrons were filled with rice, meat, vegetables and spices, then sealed and cooked over a slow fire.
10. Potato
    The word 'batata' means 'potato' in Portuguese. The Portuguese introduced potatoes in India.
11. Kakori kebab
12. Barfi
13. Jammu and Kashmir
14. Bread
15. Tamil Nadu
    It is believed to be one of the spiciest cuisines of India.
16. An oven
17. Rasam
    It is a thin, spicy south Indian soup from Tamil Nadu.
18. Mango
19. Sanjeev Kapoor
20. Fish
    Bombay duck is the English name for what is known as *bombil* in Maharashtra. It was called bummalo by the British.

INDIAN HISTORY

1. Charkha
2. Nadir Shah
3. Lord Mahavira
4. Kolkata
   Kolkata originally comprised three villages, namely Gobindapur, Sutanuti and Kalikata.
5. Swami Vivekananda
6. Mahatma Gandhi
7. Tiger
8. Kara
9. Chaitanya Mahaprabhu
   He was a Hindu mystic, whose method of worshipping the god Krishna involved ecstatic song and dance. This had a profound effect on Vaishnavism in Bengal.
10. He was conferred with the title of Raja.
11. Chola
12. Joseph Francois Dupleix
13. Rig Veda
14. Fa-Hien
15. Rajagriha
   Now called Rajgir, the city is located in the state of Bihar.
16. Ministry of Information and Broadcasting
17. Mira Bai
18. Slave
19. Ashoka
20. Swami Vivekananda

INDIAN LEADERS

1. Jawaharlal Nehru
   He served from 15 August 1947 to 27 May 1964.

2. B.R. Ambedkar
3. The Jallianwala Bagh massacre
4. C. Rajagopalachari
5. Lal Bahadur Shastri
6. Die in office
   He became the President of India on 13 May 1967 and held the office till his death on 3 May 1969.
7. Subhas Chandra Bose
8. Rajiv Gandhi
   Sadbhavna Diwas is observed on 20 August and Anti-Terrorism Day is observed on 21 May.
9. *Jai Vigyan*
10. Dadabhai Naoroji
    He was the first ever Asian to be a British Member of Parliament.
11. Science
12. Charan Singh
    He was in office from 28 July 1979 to 14 January 1980.
13. Vijaya Lakshmi Pandit
14. A.P.J. Abdul Kalam
15. Manmohan Singh
16. Mahatma Gandhi
    Gandhi wrote *The Story of My Experiments with Truth*.
17. Vallabhbhai Patel
18. Abul Kalam Azad
    National Education Day is observed every year on 11 November.
19. S. Radhakrishnan
    He was also the vice chancellor and chancellor of Banaras Hindu University (1939–48) and the University of Delhi (1953–62) respectively.
20. Rajendra Prasad

1. Premchand
2. Akela
3. Bangladesh
   Adopted in 1971, it is called *'Amar Shonar Bangla'*, which translates to 'My Golden Bengal'.
4. *Panchatantra*
   Panchatantra is the oldest work available in its original form. On the basis of internal and external clues, it can be traced all the way back to 300 BCE.
5. G. Sankara Kurup
   He received it in 1965.
6. Mandalas
   Each mandala is divided into several sections called *anuvakas*.
7. Gautama Buddha
   The word *jataka* means 'birth' in Sanskrit and Pali.
8. The Ramayana
   Around 300 original Ramayanas have been composed in Sanskrit as well as in several regional languages of India since Sage Valmiki first composed his epic.
9. *The Guide*
10. *Raghuvansham*
11. The Natyashastra
    It is believed to have been written by a Brahman sage named Bharata.
12. Bharatendu Harishchandra
13. Munshi Premchand
    Premchand's literary career started as a freelancer in Urdu.
14. Sarojini Naidu

15. Amrita Pritam
    The film starred Urmila Matondkar and Manoj Bajpayee in the lead roles.
16. *A Suitable Boy*
    Set in the early 1950s, this work was written by Vikram Seth. It is considered one of the longest novels ever published in a single volume in the English language.
17. Shiva and Parvati
    The work is about the birth of Kumara Kartikeya.
18. Ruskin Bond
19. Scorpion
20. The Ramayana

INTERNATIONAL FILMS

1. Charlie Chaplin
   He appeared on the cover in 1925.
2. Star Wars
3. Spaghetti Western
4. Bhanu Athaiya
   They received it for Richard Attenborough's *Gandhi.*
5. Satyajit Ray
6. *The Hurt Locker*
7. Martial arts
8. Ronald and Nancy Reagan
   Ronald Reagan played the role of Casey Abbott while Nancy played the role of Nurse Lt Helen Blair (as Nancy Davis).
9. Steven Spielberg
   He received the Department of Defense Medal for Distinguished Public Service for his 1998 film *Saving Private Ryan.* The movie sparked national awareness of the sacrifices made during World War II.

10. Sherlock Holmes
11. Harper Lee
12. *Iron Man*
13. *Gandhi*
    Richard Attenborough won the Oscars for Best Picture and Best Director for this film.
14. James Bond
15. Arnold Schwarzenegger
16. A reel of film
17. Ben Kingsley
    The film was based on a book by Thomas Keneally.
18. Star Wars
    The phrase originated in *Star Wars: Episode IV- A New Hope*, and has continued to be an integral part of Star Wars stories ever since.
19. *The Ten Commandments*
    It was directed by Cecil B. DeMille.
20. *Jaws*
    It was released in 1975.

KINGS AND QUEENS

1. He hid in a basket of sweets.
2. Ashoka
3. Rani Lakshmibai
4. Kushana
5. Harshavardhana
6. Chola
   The dynasty emerged in the middle of the ninth century.
7. Alauddin Khilji

8. The Koh-i-noor diamond
    It was mined from the Rayalaseema diamond mine when it
    was under the rule of the Kakatiya dynasty.
9. Bindusara
10. Maurya
    The empire reigned from about 321 BCE to 185 BCE. It grew in
    the wake of Alexander the Great's death.
11. West Bengal
    The Battle of Plassey marked the start of nearly two centuries
    of British rule in India.
12. Nadir Shah
    He founded the Iranian Empire, which stretched from the
    Indus River to the Caucasus Mountains.
13. Ghiyasuddin Balban
14. Chandragupta Maurya
    Chanakya was instrumental in helping Chandragupta
    overthrow the powerful Nanda dynasty in Pataliputra.
15. Alauddin Khilji
    The Chittorgarh Fort stands atop a 180-metre-high hill and is
    spread across 700 acres.
16. Chetak
17. Razia Sultan
    However, shortly after she ascended the throne, the nobles
    revolted against her and made her brother Muiz-ud-Din
    Bahram Shah sit on the throne.
18. Madurai
19. Shivaji
20. Harshavardhana

1. Mandarin
2. Simile
   It is used to make a description more emphatic or vivid (e.g. as brave as a lion).
3. Full stop
4. Paul
   The phrase means to take something away from one person to pay another.
5. Bibliophile
6. Equine
7. An expert at solving crossword puzzles
8. Moss
   The proverb means that a person who does not settle in one place will not accumulate wealth or status, nor responsibilities or commitments.
9. Based upon trust rather than law
10. Scrooge
11. Colon
    This punctuation mark (:) is used to precede a list of items, a quotation or an expansion or explanation.
12. Epitaph
13. Drey
    It is typically in the form of a mass of twigs in a tree.
14. Term used for a person who watches a lot of TV with no exercise
15. Eggs of a small shark
16. Omega
    The twenty-fourth, and last, letter of the Greek alphabet is written as Ω in uppercase and ω in lowercase.

17. A graveyard, because of the marble tombstones
18. Chit
19. Securing official documents with red or pink tape
20. Ampersand

LEADERS OF THE WORLD

1. Margaret Thatcher
She was the only British prime minister in the twentieth century to win three consecutive terms.
2. Abraham Lincoln
In November 1863, Abraham Lincoln was invited to deliver a speech, which later came to be known as the Gettysburg Address.
3. Juan Perón
He was the President of Argentina for three terms (1946–52, 1952–55 and 1973–74).
4. Carter
They were Howard Carter and Jimmy Carter respectively.
5. Joseph Stalin
He died in 1953.
6. Turkey
In 1923, Turkey became a secular republic with Atatürk as its President.
7. Israel
8. Aung San Suu Kyi
9. Liberia
The capital city is Monrovia.
10. Mao Zedong
11. Clement Attlee
12. Angela Merkel

13. Yitzhak Rabin
    He was the prime minister of Israel and led peace negotiations with Palestine and neighbouring Arab countries.
14. Nelson Mandela
15. Lenin
    He was the first head of the Soviet states (1917–24).
16. Franklin Roosevelt
17. Sheikh Hasina Wazed
18. Adolf Hitler
19. Literature
20. Napoleon

MIXED BAG

1. *Pather Panchali*
   It was based on a novel by Bibhutibhushan Bandyopadhyay.
2. Coffee
3. Genius
4. Bhutan
5. Macbeth
6. *Mr Natwarlal*
7. Feet
8. Shabana Azmi
9. Hercule Poirot
   The detective features in a series of novels by Agatha Christie.
10. Newspaper
11. Pandit Ravi Shankar
    Ravi Shankar was an Indian musician and composer, best known for popularizing the sitar and Indian classical music in Western culture.
12. A British prison camp

13. *Victory*

    Before the Battle of Trafalgar, he delivered the famous message, 'England expects that every man will do his duty.'
14. Santa Claus
15. Maharashtra
16. Nutmeg
17. *Panchatantra*
18. Diamond
19. Jigsaw puzzles
20. Bhagat Singh

    He was a good journalist. He contributed to many newspapers, including *Kirti*, *Akali*, *Arjun* and *Pratap*.

MOUNTAINS AND HILLS

1. Sir George Everest, the then surveyor general of India

   It was referred to as Peak XV before 1865.
2. Kilimanjaro

   It is located in north-eastern Tanzania, near the border of Kenya.
3. Fuji

   The highest mountain in Japan, it is a volcano that last erupted in 1707.
4. Andes

   The Andes comprise the highest peaks in the western hemisphere.
5. Krishna
6. Sweets
7. Aravalli
8. Heidi

   Published in the 1880s, the story vividly describes the mountain pastures and Heidi's simple life there.

9. Kamakhya Temple
   It was built in honour of Sati, an incarnation of Goddess Durga or Goddess Shakti.
10. Asia
11. Kanchenjunga
    It is situated on the border between north-eastern India and eastern Nepal.
12. Khyber Pass
13. Tenzing Norgay
    This book was also published as *Man of Everest* in 1955.
14. Mauna Loa
    It is located on the island of Hawaii, USA.
15. Karnataka
16. The carved heads of four US Presidents
    The four Presidents are George Washington, Thomas Jefferson, Abraham Lincoln and Theodore Roosevelt.
17. The Karakoram
18. Doddabetta
    It is in the Nilgiri mountain range, at the junction of the Western and Eastern Ghats.
19. Turkey
20. Siachen Glacier

MUGHALS

1. Taj Mahal
2. Aurangzeb
   Born Muhi ud-Din Muhammad on 3 November 1618, he is considered to be the last of the great Mughal emperors.
3. Nur Jahan was Mumtaz Mahal's aunt.
4. Zafar

5. Nur Jahan
   Shalimar Bagh is located in Jammu and Kashmir. The garden was divided into three terraced sections for different purposes.
6. Pakistan
7. Shah Jahan
8. Akbar
9. Myanmar
   Bahadur Shah Zafar was eighty-two years old at the time.
10. Birbal
11. Babur
12. Nur Jahan
13. Red Fort
    The throne was built for Mughal emperor Shah Jahan in the early seventeenth century.
14. Sher Shah Suri
15. Todar Mal
    He was one of the Navratnas of Akbar's court.
16. Humayun
17. Babur
18. Uttar Pradesh
    It was built during the second half of the sixteenth century and served as the capital of the Mughal Empire for about ten years.
19. Agra Fort
20. Shah Jahan

MUSIC

1. Ravi Shankar
2. Ghatam
   It is a large, narrow-mouthed earthenware water-pot used as a percussion instrument.

3. To pluck the strings of his musical instrument
4. Satyajit Ray
   The film is based on a story by Upendrakishore Ray Chowdhury.
5. Zakir Hussain
   He is the son of Ustad Allarakha Khan.
6. Rebab
   The rebab came into use in the Arab world around the eighth century.
7. Lata Mangeshkar
8. Santoor
9. Pink Floyd
   The band was named after Pink Anderson and Floyd Council.
10. Trumpet
11. Backstreet Boys
12. Flute
    The musical text *Sangeet Ratnakar*, written in the thirteenth century by Sharangdeva, refers to eighteen kinds of flutes. These categories are based on the distance between the blow hole and the first finger hole.
13. Mukhda
14. Mridangam
15. M.S. Subbulakshmi
16. Michael Jackson
17. Shiv Kumar Sharma
    Pandit Shiv Kumar Sharma is an eminent santoor player; Pandit Hariprasad Chaurasia is a flautist.
18. Kishore Kumar
19. Paul McCartney
20. Wajid Ali Shah

1. Border Security Force
   It was founded in 1965.
2. Greenpeace
   Greenpeace India was founded in 2001.
3. Indian Coast Guard
   It was formally constituted in August 1978 under the Coast Guard Act, 1978.
4. Blue
5. Petroleum
   OPEC stands for Organization of the Petroleum Exporting Countries.
6. The Gestapo
7. Amnesty International
   The organization began with British lawyer Peter Benenson writing an article in a newspaper and launching a campaign.
8. New York City
9. The Indian Army
10. The five continents joined in the Olympic Movement
    The rings on the flag were suggested by French educator Pierre de Coubertin.
11. Mahatma Gandhi
12. It also stood for the initials (BP) of its founder.
13. Indian Railways
14. The National Cadet Corps
15. Kofi Annan
16. Giant panda
17. CRPF
18. World War I
19. The USA

20. Uruguay
It was organized in 1930.

PHYSICS

1. It is in a sealed, oxygen-free chamber.
2. Salt
Salt lowers the freezing/melting point of water. Thus large amounts of salt are used in countries like Canada to help rid thoroughfares of accumulated snow and ice.
3. Anemometer
4. Paper
5. Microwave oven
6. An equal and opposite reaction
7. Sublimation
8. Loses electrons
9. Algorithm
10. −40 degrees
11. Pumping water
12. Spectrum
13. Hardness of minerals
It was devised by German mineralogist Friedrich Mohs.
14. 'Mary Had a Little Lamb'
The phonograph was developed as a result of Thomas Edison's work on two other inventions, the telegraph and the telephone.
15. The moon
16. $E=mc^2$
17. Leonardo da Vinci
18. Momentum
The larger the mass and velocity, the greater the momentum.

19. Ammeter

20. Simple

PLANTS AND TREES

1. Neem

2. Bamboo

3. Sandalwood

4. Quinine

Quinine was first synthesized in a laboratory in 1944.

5. Ginger

6. Saffron

It is an orange-yellow flavouring, food colouring and dye made from the dried stigmas of a crocus.

7. Rubber tree

8. Coir

9. Alphonso

10. Eucalyptus

11. Jute

It is one of nature's strongest vegetable fibres.

12. Rice

13. Tea

According to legend, tea has been cultivated in China since about 2700 BCE.

14. Linen

15. Grape

16. Peepul tree

It is also called the Bodhi tree.

17. The finger

18. Clove

19. Inner bark

20. Teak

1. Uttar Pradesh
2. New Zealand
   The women of New Zealand first went to the polls in the national elections of November 1893.
3. Vice president
4. Kitchen cabinet
5. The Governor
6. The Constitution of India
   The Constituent Assembly took two years, eleven months and seventeen days to complete the historic task of drafting the Constitution for independent India.
7. East Timor
   The country gained independence on 20 May 2002.
8. The attorney general
9. Sri Lanka
   It is located in the south-western part of the country, about 8 kilometres south-east of the commercial capital of Colombo.
10. One-third
11. The prime minister
12. 11 Downing Street
13. Indelible ink
    Inaugurated in 1937, the factory was set up by the then royal family of Mysore (now Mysuru).
14. The Indian National Congress
    It was founded on 28 December 1885, and played a major role in India's freedom struggle.
15. Amitabh Bachchan
16. Morarji Desai

17. Question Hour

It is during Question Hour that members of the house may ask questions about different aspects of administration and government policy in the national as well as international spheres.

18. Delhi
19. The vice president
20. Oval Office

SCIENTISTS

1. C.V. Raman
2. Albert Einstein
3. Samuel Morse
4. Logarithms
5. Louis Pasteur

He was considered one of the most important founders of medical microbiology.

6. Ruthenium

The name is derived from Ruthenia, the Latin name for Russia.

7. Pierre and Marie Curie
8. Isaac Newton
9. Thomas Alva Edison
10. Subrahmanyan Chandrasekhar

This observatory observes many things, including black holes and high-temperature gases throughout the X-ray portion of the electromagnetic spectrum.

11. Meghnad Saha
12. Homi Bhabha
13. Antoine Lavoisier

He realized its capability to form acids by combining with many different substances, and so he called the element 'oxygen'. The word comes from the Greek words for 'acid former'.

14. Telephone

Alexander Graham Bell conducted a successful experiment with the telephone on 10 March 1876.

15. Penicillin

16. Humphry Davy

17. Benjamin Franklin

Franklin told George Whatley, his friend, that he'd found them extremely useful at a dinner in France. With the help of the lenses, he could see the food he was eating and watch the facial expressions of those seated at the table with him.

18. Politics

19. They were both deaf.

20. Kala-azar

SPORTS

1. Dhyan Chand

He is considered one of the greatest hockey players of all time.

2. The advent of colour television in India

3. P.T. Usha

Pilavullakandi Thekkeparambil Usha is a retired Indian track-and-field athlete.

4. Karate

5. Leander Paes

6. Penhold grip

Using this grip, the player holds the table tennis bat in a downward-pointing direction.

7. Rubik's Cube

It was invented by Erno Rubik.

8. High jump
9. Football
10. She allegedly stole a flag from the Japanese Imperial Palace. Shortly after the 1964 Olympics, the Australian Swimming Union banned her for ten years, bringing her competitive career to an end.
11. Tennis
   It was first presented to the Wimbledon champion when the challenge round was introduced in 1886.
12. The 1936 Berlin Olympics
13. Muhammad Ali
14. Basketball
15. Hockey
16. Billy Jean King
   The match was known as the Battle of the Sexes.
17. Decathlon
18. Polo
19. Basketball
20. The soldiers were not concentrating on archery.

SUPERLATIVES

1. Mira Bai
2. Qutub Minar
3. Kiwi
4. Mark Twain
   The book was *Life on the Mississippi*, published in 1883.
5. Mount Everest
   In 1865, the mountain, previously referred to as Peak XV, was renamed for Sir George Everest, the British surveyor general of India from 1830 to 1843.

6. Aishwarya Rai
7. Largest state in terms of area
8. Fairy Queen
9. Asha Bhosle
10. Africa
    The Nile is the world's longest river and the Sahara is the world's largest hot desert.
11. Florence Nightingale
12. Baikal
    It is located in the southern part of eastern Siberia.
13. Climb Mount Everest
14. Satyendranath Tagore
    He was allotted Bombay Presidency Cadre.
15. Amazon
    The length of the river is equivalent to the distance from New York City to Rome.
16. Linus Pauling
    He received the 1954 Nobel Prize in Chemistry and the 1962 Nobel Peace Prize.
17. Stops
    It has 115 halts.
18. Silver
19. Muhammad Ali
20. Mawsynram
    The average annual rainfall in Mawsynram is 11,873 millimetres, whereas that in Cherrapunji is 11,430 millimetres.

THE GREAT EPICS I

1. Dasharatha
2. Conch shell

3. Indra

   The vajra made a scar on his *hanu,* or jawbone. So the devas named him Hanuman.

4. Ass

5. Meghnad

   He was the son of Ravana and Mandodari.

6. Sita

7. Sabari

   She was Malini, a *gandharva* woman, in her previous birth.

8. Gandhari

9. Ravana

10. Shanta

11. Sugriva

    He entered into an alliance with Rama and helped him rescue Sita.

12. Veda Vyasa

13. Balarama

    He was the elder brother of Krishna.

14. Jambavan

15. Pushpaka Vimana

    Ravana had taken the chariot from Kubera.

16. Kaikeyi

17. Jaya

    The Mahabharata is also known as the Bharatasamhita.

18. Sahadeva

    Shakuni was Gandhari's brother.

19. Trijata

20. Abhimanyu

1. Dussala
2. Narada
   He related to Valmiki a brief history of Rama.
3. Ganesha
4. Ravana
5. Ganga
6. Dance and music teacher
   He adopted the name Brihannala and became tutor to Princess Uttara.
7. Dasharatha
8. Karna
9. Shatrughna
10. Vibhishana
    He had advised Ravana to free Sita.
11. Takshaka
    Takshaka entered the palace inside a fruit, disguised as a worm.
12. Mareecha
    He was Ravana's uncle.
13. Bhima
    Their son was Ghatotkacha.
14. Shiva
15. Arjuna
16. Saraswati
17. Bhishma
18. Valmiki
19. Arjuna
20. Dhrishtadyumna
    He was Draupadi's brother.

1. Taj Mahal
2. Famine relief project
   The Bada Imambara was built by Nawab Asaf-ud-Daulah and designed by Kifayat-ullah.
3. Munshi Premchand
4. Gateway of India
5. The end of the plague
6. Trams
7. It was coloured pink for the Prince of Wales's (King Edward VII) visit in 1876.
8. Qutub Minar
9. Lord Krishna's crown
10. Chariot
11. Khajuraho
    It is a village in Madhya Pradesh.
12. Chhatrapati Shivaji
    It is one of the busiest railway stations in the country.
13. The Calcutta Metro
14. Taj Mahal
15. Lotus Temple
16. Uttar Pradesh
17. Chandigarh
18. Elephanta Caves
    The Elephanta Caves are located on an island about 10 kilometres from Mumbai.
19. India Gate
20. Golden Temple

1. The German Secret State Police during World War II
2. Alexander the Great
   The Battle of Gaugamela is also called the Battle of Arbela.
3. The Crimean War
4. Harry S. Truman
   On 12 April 1945, he became America's thirty-third President.
5. The French Revolution
   It is also called the Revolution of 1789, and it denotes the end of the Ancien Régime in France.
6. A tank
   It was the main battle tank designed and built by the United States for World War II.
7. Ashoka
8. Belgium
   The defeat of Napoleon at Waterloo marked the end of his military adventures.
9. The Bastille
   Originally built as a medieval fortress, it was often used to hold political prisoners captive, just as citizens were detained there by authorities for trial.
10. Siraj-ud-Daulah
11. World War I
12. Babur
13. Sir Winston Churchill
14. Tipu Sultan
15. William the Conqueror
    It was fought on Senlac Hill, about 11 kilometres from Hastings. King Harold II was the last Anglo-Saxon king of England.

16. Adolf Hitler

With the death of German President Paul von Hindenburg, chancellor Adolf Hitler became the absolute dictator of Germany under the title of führer.

17. His arm

In July 1797, Nelson led an assault on the Spanish island of Tenerife, during which he was hit in the right arm by a musket ball.

18. Rajasthan

19. The Hiroshima bombing

The aircraft was named after the mother of pilot Paul Warfield Tibbets Jr.

20. Panipat

WORDPLAY

1. Kleptomaniac

It comes from the Greek word *kleptes*, meaning 'thief'.

2. 'Thank you very much'

It is in French.

3. Loot

4. Sailor

5. Fortress

6. Bonsai

It is the art of training and growing trees in containers.

7. Dolphin

8. Ski

9. Druid

10. Lullaby

11. Crawled

12. New Year's

13. Health
14. Karaoke
    It is a form of entertainment in which people take turns to sing popular songs into a microphone, over pre-recorded backing tracks.
15. A type of Japanese poem
    It is a poem of seventeen syllables, in three lines of five, seven and five syllables respectively.
16. 'To be licked'
17. Gold
    Bullion is gold or silver in bulk (before coining), El Dorado is a fictitious country or city abounding in gold and California is famous for its Gold Rush.
18. Catch animals illegally
19. Monkeys
20. 'The sun has stopped'
    These are the times in the year, in the middle of the summer or winter, when we have the longest hours of day or night.

WORLD CUISINE

1. Pie
   A pizza is a large circle of flat bread baked with cheese, tomatoes and sometimes meat and vegetables spread on top.
2. Falafel
3. Chop suey
   It is a dish prepared chiefly with bean sprouts, bamboo shoots, water chestnuts, onions, mushrooms and meat or fish, and served with rice and soya sauce.
4. Pasta
   Pasta is usually associated with Italian cuisine.

5. It came from Hamburg in Germany.
6. Deer
7. Frankfurter
8. Tabasco
9. Marco Polo
   He brought back descriptions of fruit ices from his travels in China.
10. Pestle
    A pestle is a heavy tool with a rounded end, used for crushing and grinding substances such as spices or drugs, typically in a mortar.
11. Biscuit
    Originally biscuits were made using a twofold process: they were baked first and then dried out in a slow oven.
12. Hot cross bun
    These buns are marked with a cross and have dried fruit.
13. Sushi
14. Sundae
15. A crescent-shaped roll
16. Cheese
17. Shrimp
18. The Championships, Wimbledon
19. Oliver Twist
20. Spun sugar on a stick

WORLD GEOGRAPHY

1. The atlas
   Gerardus Mercator was a Flemish cartographer who developed a map with what was later known as the Mercator

projection. He also introduced the term 'atlas' for a collection of maps.

2. Kalahari
3. Indonesia
   Some seventy-six are historically active.
4. Istanbul
5. The Amazon rainforest
   The Amazon rainforest has an extremely rich ecosystem. It has 40,000 plant species, 1300 bird species, 3000 types of fish, 430 types of mammals and 2.5 million different insects.
6. Chinook
7. Angel
   Located in Venezuela, it is the highest waterfall in the world.
8. The Grand Canyon
9. Wellington
   It is the capital of New Zealand, located in the extreme south of North Island.
10. Tanzania
    It is an East African country situated just south of the equator.
11. Ayers Rock
    Surveyor William Gosse named it for Sir Henry Ayers, former South Australian premier.
12. Brazil
13. Nile
    The Nile basin includes parts of Ethiopia, Sudan, Tanzania, Burundi, Rwanda, the Democratic Republic of the Congo, Kenya, Uganda, South Sudan and certain areas of Egypt.
14. Q
15. Russia
16. Taiwan
17. Mount Fuji

18. Argentina

The Latin word for silver is *argentum*. Argentina is a great source of this mineral.

19. Buddhism

20. Tortoise

The Spanish word for tortoise is *galápago*.

WORLD HISTORY

1. Three hundred and forty-two chests of tea were dumped into the Boston Harbour by demonstrators.

2. *Golden Hind*

The ship was originally called *The Pelican* and weighed about 100 tons.

3. Abraham Lincoln

He was only nineteen years old when the incident happened.

4. Truth

5. Pakistan

6. Ferdinand Magellan

The Portuguese navigator and explorer sailed under the flags of both Portugal and Spain.

7. Martin Luther King Jr

8. Winston Churchill

On 2 June 1953, Queen Elizabeth II was formally crowned monarch of the United Kingdom.

9. Confucius

10. Cleopatra

She ruled with her son Ptolemy XV Caesar.

11. Genghis Khan

12. Karl Marx

These words were spoken by the German philosopher to his housekeeper after she asked if he had any last words.

13. Fiddle

    The fire lasted for six days and seven nights. Seventy per cent of the city was destroyed during this fire.
14. The Statue of Liberty

    This extract is taken from the sonnet 'The New Colossus' by Emma Lazarus.
15. 150
16. Alexander
17. Vasco da Gama

    St Francis Church was the first European church to be built in India.
18. Egypt
19. All were assassinated.
20. Oslo

WORLD LITERATURE

1. Limerick
2. O. Henry

    He was an American short story writer, whose tales romanticized the commonplace.
3. Cat

    The cat is also called the Hidden Paw as he is a criminal mastermind who disregards the law.
4. Ian Fleming
5. Hercule Poirot
6. Rudyard Kipling

    He was forty-one years old when he was awarded the Nobel Prize in Literature in 1907.
7. Lewis Carroll

8. *Les Misérables*
   The novel is set in the Parisian underworld and plotted like a detective story.
9. *Hamlet*
10. *1984*
11. Sherlock Holmes
    Holmes first appeared in Conan Doyle's *A Study in Scarlet*, published in *Beeton's Christmas Annual* of 1887.
12. Leo Tolstoy
13. *Gulliver's Travels*
14. George Orwell
15. *Gitanjali*
    The collection of poems was written by Rabindranath Tagore.
16. V.S. Naipaul
    This book was the first to bring Naipaul worldwide acclaim.
17. H.H. Munro
18. Antonio
19. Robin Hood
20. *Pygmalion*

WORLD MYTHS

1. It could rise from its ashes after burning itself.
2. Killing the Nemean lion
   It was Eurystheus who imposed upon Hercules the famous Labours.
3. A winged infant with a bow and arrows
   Cupid is the Roman god of love.
4. Argus

5. Iris
   She is the personification of the rainbow as well as a messenger of the gods.
6. Thor
7. Sun
8. Pan
   He was associated with the pastoral god Faunus by the Romans.
9. Mars
10. Olympus
11. Jackal
    Also called Anpu, Anubis is the ancient Egyptian god of the dead.
12. Pandora
    In Greek mythology, she is the first mortal woman.
13. Mnemosyne
    The name comes from the Greek word *mnemosune*, which literally means 'memory'.
14. King Arthur
15. Her voice remained
16. Valkyrie
17. Midas
18. Egypt
19. His heel
    According to some, Thetis dipped Achilles in the waters of the Styx River, which made him invincible—except for his heel, by which she'd held him while dipping him.
20. Medusa

WORLD TOUR

1. The Leaning Tower of Pisa
    Piazza dei Miracoli or the Square of Miracles is a walled area in Pisa, Italy.
2. Belgium
3. International orange
4. Australia
    It has about 400 types of corals, 1500 species of fish and 4000 types of molluscs.
5. The Statue of Liberty
    Since the pedestal for the statue was not complete when the ship arrived, the structure was reassembled on Bedloe's Island only in 1886.
6. Little Mermaid
7. The pyramids of Giza
    Located in Egypt, these are the massive tombs of Egyptian pharaohs.
8. Kilimanjaro
9. Venice
    It is built over the Rio di Palazzo canal between the Doge's Palace and the prisons. It gets its name from the 'sighs' of the prisoners who passed over it.
10. New York City
11. John Lennon
12. Bangkok
13. Berlin
    When Berlin was divided in 1961, the main crossing point between east and west was at Checkpoint Charlie.
14. Italy

15. The Colosseum

16. Kyat

One kyat is equal to 100 pyas.

17. The Sydney Harbour Bridge

It is known by locals as the Coat Hanger because of its arch-based design.

18. The Eiffel Tower

It was built by Gustave Eiffel.

19. The White House

It is the office and official residence of the President of the United States of America.

20. Niagara Falls

The falls comprise two principal parts separated by Goat Island.

ACKNOWLEDGEMENTS

When you conduct a quiz contest for twenty-five long years, as the quizmaster, you tend to get all the credit and accolades. I am deeply grateful for all the love and respect that I have received from the millions who have grown up watching this iconic show. Even today, I am truly touched and proud when some viewers still—in their thirties and forties—come up to me and gush about how much they enjoyed the show.

But to produce a quality show like this, over such a long period of time, you need a rock solid team that is committed, passionate, hard-working, dedicated and resilient.

The credit needs to be shared.

At the risk of leaving someone out, here is a list of people who, for a quarter of a century, worked tirelessly in the background to make the multiple-award-winning *Bournvita Quiz Contest* the most watched and followed English-language game show in the history of Indian television.

Directors
Derek O'Brien
Gyan Sahay

Online Editors/Directors
Dongrej Gor

Offline Editors
Bhavin Patel
Kshitij Rajkumar
Siddharth Bhura
Vivek Iyer

Directors of Photography
Gyan Sahay
R. Diwakaran
Sathyanarayan

Assistants to DOP
Selvam J.
Selvaraj Xavier

Sound
Ashwyn Balsaver
Madanlal
Seby Fernandes
Sivadas

Music
Leslie Lewis
Shankar–Ehsaan–Loy

Producer
Rila Banerjee

Sound and Lights
Friends of Shiva

Hindi Script
Rajneesh Kaushal

Executive Producers
Andrew Scolt
Arindam Roy Choudhury
Debkumar Mitra
Kalyanmoy Hazra
Mahua Basu
Nayan Chaudhury
Prabuddha Chatterjee
R.P. Chatterjee
Sanjay Sachdeva
Sukanya Mukherjee
Sunil Shah
Supreah Sawhny
Tess Joseph
Vinayak Das

Production Associates
Aanya O'Brien
Dana Roy
Jinu Joseph
Mariam Munir
Michael Blacquiere

Raksha Burman
Shamajita Chatterjee
Shane Baptiste
Sharmishta Chatterjee
Sreevalsa Menon
Supriyo Nandi
Victor Bhat
Vikash Rai
Vinu Joseph

Research Associates
Abhishkta Banerjee
Amartya Pathak
Amit Ghosh
Ammar Hamid
Amrita Sadhukhan
Angana Ghosh
Anik Ghosal
Anushtup Haldar
Arnab Das
Arpita Sinha
Arundhati Bhattacharya
Arupratan Chakraborty
Ayashman Dey
Barnali Chatterjee
Bidisha Paul
Binita Roy
Debaroti Chakraborty
Debjani Sen
Deepa Vachhani
Devarshi Ghosh

Fatema Marfatia
Fiona Fernandez
Grenville Daunt
Indrani Bhattacharya
Malavika
Mark Cranenburgh
Mayuri Dutta Chowdhury
Neil French
Nilanjana Basu
Philip Antunis
Rudradeep Bhattacharjee
Sanchita Agarwal
Sankha Ganguli
Sarbajit Ghosh
Saurav Dey
Shalini Chaudhury
Sharmistha Dutta
Shubhayu Sengupta
Simon Jennings
Sreevalsa Menon
Srirupa Roy
Sugandha Kapoor
Suman Ray
Sushmita Dutta
Sylvia Eugene
Tanushankar
Vipul Rathore

Co-Anchors
Moushumi Saha
Niall Sadh

Nisha Krishnan
Saumya Tandon
Shonal Rawat

Designers
Anushkaa Basu
Niladri Das
Pratapaditya Sarkar

Finance Associates
Devika Chowdhury
Kaushal Tiwari
Pinaki Nag
Snehasish Sarkar
Vikash Parasrampuria

Production Assistants
Arjun
Bipin Kumar Jha
Dilip Rai
Indrajit Saha
Mrinal Chakraborty
Pabitra Ghosh
Saikat Dey
Sudip Roy

IT Associates
Claude Franklin
Debashish Mondal
Kaushik Majumder
M. Suresh

Rajkumar Sreevastava
Sagar Sengupta
Shaikat Das
Sharmila Singh

Relationship Associates
A.V.N.S. Prasad
Aanchal Bali
Aashrita Abraham
Abhijit Sanyal
Abhisek Roy
Agnes Thoompunkal
Ahona Ghosh
Alina Shirazi
Ameya Dabli
Andre D'Cruz
Andrew Antunis
Anita Ganguli
Anjali Kanwar
Arun Malaviya
Ashish Daga
Aubrey Whyte
Avik Lee
Baishali Chatterjee
Bhavish Gamage
Bhavisha Sandhya
Bhavna Khosla
Bindu Unnithan
Boris Anthony
Calvin Tully
Candice Cooper

Chetan Mathur
Christopher Crouch
Conrad Pote
Daniel Johns
Darren Ross
Debarun Roychoudhary
Debashish Dutta
Debjani Banerjee
Dennis Rozario
Dhanashekhar
Dipankar Rao
Divisha Chandna
Donford Goves
Donovin Grant
Doyson Gomes
Durjoy Guha
Dyu D'Cunha
Edward Berger
Elvis Fernandes
Ezekiel Mani
Ferhana Jila
Fionna Sayers
Gaurav Ajmera
Gaurav Paul
Gayathri Acharya
Gloria Gomes
Harish V.
Heena Ade
Hitasha Singla
Ishita Bose Chakraborty
Jacqueline Hale

James Norman
Jasmine Batra
Jason Pote
Jean Attick
Jeffrey D'Cruize
Johann Palmer
John Bhatia
Jwalant Dixit
Jyoti Dhawan
K. Vijay Kumar
Keya Dutta
Kumkum Tandon
Laressa Gomez
Lisha Nair
Luke Mani
Lyndon Gomes
Mahesh Makhija
Mita Bannerjee
Nancy DuPratt
Nancy Sebastian
Natalia Scen
Natasha Gasper
Neil Bullock
Nitin Naik
Obrie McDonald
Padmavati Nori
Parul Yadav
Patricia Pattison
Payal Patange
Prashant Pillai
Prateek Mehrotra

Preeti Anand
Pritha Ghosh
Priya Khanna
Ragupati P
Rahul Kumar
Rajarshi Gupta
Rama Venkataraman
Rashmeet Kaur Sood
Reggie Didier'Serre
Ricardo Abraham
Ricardo Bosco
Rini Nandy
Rohit Jain
Ruchi Sengur
Rumeli Chakraborty
Runu Mehta
Ryan Price
Sanat Tandon
Sargam Sekri
Sean Augustine
Severin Coates Reid
Shailly Jindal
Shamik Chakraborty
Shane Alliew
Shane Pratchett
Shaoni Chowdhury
Shaun Ward
Sheldon Alliew

Sherman Alliew
Shivani Kapur
Shivani Sarathi
Shyam S. Latha
Simran Puri
Sita Srinivas
Smitha D'Souza
Sonal Kamat
Sonal Suvarna
Sonali Menzes Sequeira
Sowmya Pratapa
Stephen Samuel
Stuti Singh
Sudha Anand
Sudipta Dhruva
Sujatha Sadananda
Sushmita Malaviya
T. Venkatasubramaniam
Tamanna Ahuja
Tapan Roy
Thiruchengottaian
Tunir Kumar
V. Sree Madhuri
Valentina Burgess
Vijayanti Rana
Vishakha Chatterjee
Walter Philips
Yasmeen C.B.

We fondly remember the late James Norman and Amala Thomas.

All good things must come to an end. It's been a glorious and fulfilling twenty-five years. It's goodbye from the *Bournvita Quiz Contest* for now. May it remain an everlasting memory.

READ MORE BY THE SAME AUTHOR

The Best of Cadbury Bournvita Quiz Contest

For saving whose life was Nazm, a water bearer, crowned king for half a day at Agra Fort?

The literal meaning of which term in Latin is 'and the rest'?

Which Indian prime minister made a brief appearance in the 1977 film *Chala Murari Hero Ban Ne*?

How is muriatic acid better known?

Here are 1000 of the very best questions ever asked at the popular *Cadbury Bournvita Quiz Contest*!

It started as a radio quiz programme in 1972 and went on to become one of the most sought-after school quizzes in the country. On overwhelming public demand, BQC makes a comeback on television in 2011 and, with it, quizmaster Derek O'Brien brings you a compilation of 1000 questions from the archives of India's longest-running television game show. And just so you can be even more of a quiz whizz, there are 100 fun facts for you to know and enjoy.

The Puffin Factfinder

Who was the first man to play golf on the moon?

Where would you weigh less—the equator or the North Pole?

What was the name of the poet known as the Parrot of India?

From Asia's best known quizmaster, Derek O'Brien, comes this ultimate reference book for students and inquisitive minds. Exhaustive and comprehensive, *The Puffin Factfinder* offers relevant information on everything you wanted to know. This handy book provides reliable and interesting information on a varied range of subjects, including history, geography, politics, science, literature, music, mathematics and more.

Here's your chance to get a low-down on anything—from historical anecdotes to global warming, the solar system to social networking. Comprising facts, figures, statistics and intriguing trivia, this indispensable reference book is ideal for schools, libraries and any quiz or trivia junkie.